Caring For Someone You Love

With Kindness, Love and Respect

Suzanne Elise Abels, M.S.

First Edition Design Publishing
Sarasota, Florida USA

Caring for Someone You Love Copyright ©2018
Suzanne Elise Abels

ISBN 978-1506-908-71-7 AMZ
ISBN 978-1506-906-01-0 PRINT
ISBN 978-1506-906-02-7 EBOOK

LCCN 2018937284

March 2018

Published and Distributed by
First Edition Design Publishing, Inc.
P.O. Box 20217, Sarasota, FL 34276-3217
www.firsteditiondesignpublishing.com

This book is dedicated to my Daddy:
Dr Gerald Gordon Comisar
Affectionately known as "Jerry."

"Love is the Bridge."
~S.E.A

Thank you to my twin brother Jamie for his strength and courage in the face of all the complicated decisions and challenges we faced in Dad's last year of life. I could not have made it without you, "JJ". Thank you, Jamie and Amber, for driving Dad from San Jose all the way down to Irvine.

Thank you to my husband, Peter, who held down the home front for 31 days when I moved up north to care for Dad. Peter read Dad the Sunday times and engaged my Dad in political conversations which Dad loved. Peter took Dad for walks several times a week, ate breakfast with him, built his furniture and ordered his supplies. He gave me breaks when I was afraid even to leave Dad for a day! You are my one true anchor in life.

Thank you to my beloved children, Zachary, Haley and Riley who supported me from afar in the hardest time of my life: you are my EVERYTHING!

Thank you to my Mom (Dad's first wife) who told countless stories of Dad as a younger man and sent him treats.

Thank you to my Uncle Mike, who spent hours listening to me sob while saying things would get better. This is the man you want on your life's team.

Thank you to my Sister-in-Law, Amber, who navigated through so many obstacles and always found the answers no one else could unearth. Amber found every possible health gadget and source known to man. She also added sunshine to Dad's life by bringing Ella, his Granddaughter, for breakfasts.

Thank you Annelise Balfour-Couchman for showing me true strength and courage. Your friendship has been a blessing and a gift.

Thank you to Flora and Dr. Jon Ahdoot, our dear friends. John was a platinum doctor and he and Flora supportive friends when Dad entered the hospital for the last 5 days of his life. Jon and Flora were a life raft in turbulent seas. Jon personally took over Dads end of life care and made my family and I comforted by his presence and attention.

Thank you to Lisa, Steve and Danny who were always available despite my tears and uncertainty. They are friends through thick and thin. They are what defines the word friendship.

Thank you to Robin "Izzy" who was 24/7 available to me for the kind of support that made this treacherous journey survivable those first few months. She is my sister in every sense of the word.

Thank you to Helen, Daniel and Lauren (Dad's second wife and kids) who gave Dad a reason to look forward to his week. Dad loved & adored all of you and saved every card and note you sent.

Thank you to the unsung heroes that were Dad's caregivers, especially Angelica, a true Angel.

Thank you to Dr. Stanton for the hours spent talking physics and mathematics to keep my dad alert.

Thank you to Jane Mundt who offered advocacy when I didn't know where to turn.

Thank you to Nina O"Neil for your spiritual sisterhood through this journey.

Thank you to my Dad's private nurses; Jean and his physical therapist, Crystal, who Dad liked so much for both their care and humor.

Thank you to my Dad's Atria best friends, Gene & Loie, who always had a kind word for Dad, a hug and a smile.

Thank you to Dads best friends in Northern California, Gordon Hamachi and Tom Anderson. Dad loved and admired you both. Gordon was one of the few people Dad would allow to visit in the senior home and mentioned it for days.

Thank you to Adele Sands and Audrey Lynch, Dad's favorite book club friends, who visited him and brought him books.

Thank you to my incredible Facebook community that rallied around me when I dropped out of sight, praying and sending notes and love.

If I forgot anyone, please know that my gratitude extends beyond these pages.

Table of Contents

My Dad, Jerry Comisar 1
The Call 2
The Lion Roared 7
Empathy...11
Miracles do Happen 15
The Secret Oasis 16
The Roller Coaster..18
An Attitude of Gratitude 19
I Love You..21
Code Blue..22
The Bunker...26
Codes, Passwords, Keys and Signature Cards are a Must!! 27
Photo Journal 32
Breathe 34
Tears are Necessary...35
Goals 37
Advocacy and its Many Hats...40
Diagnosis...43
Graduation Day for Dad!!!..46
Adjusting to a New Environment 49
The Battle for Independence..52
Friends 56
Trust Your Instincts Choosing a Skilled Nursing or Assisted Living Residence..57
Time 62
Moving Day! 63
New Beginnings in Southern California..65
Memories 69
Kindness Matters..71
It Takes a Village 73
Inspire 77
Be a Part of the Solution 78
Rite of Passage 79
The Bridge 82
One Day at a Time..83
A Physician with Compassion...85
Make Lemonade out of Lemons..87
God Places You Where You are Meant to Be (or A Fall From Grace)...............88
Be Creative 92

The Heart of the Matter is Love 93
It Ain't Easy 94
Striking a Balance.. 96
Wheelchairs.. 98
Cranes 101
Peaches... 102
Nature 103
LOVE is a Potent Balm 105
Strength 107
Dignity.. 109
Seasons.. 111
Rainbows 112
Warrior 115
Captivity 118
Caregivers.. 120
Divine Grace 122
Champagne 124
Anchor 125
Rise Up 126
Service... 127
Messages of Hope and Love... 128
Heroes... 130
Wherever You Go, There You Are!!! 131
Diplomacy 133
Thanksgiving... 134
Exhale 136
Actions Speak Louder than Words!.. 137
Say What You Need to Say... 138
Elder Abuse is Shocking!.. 139
Grief 141
Silence is Golden 143
My Angel Daughter.. 145
The Descent.. 147
Letting go.. 149
I'm Walking Dad Home 151
Epilogue.. 152
On Death - Gibran... 159
About the Author 160

A note from the author

My nonfiction, self-help book, *Caring for Someone You Love*, deals with helping my father during the last year of his life. Healthy and active all his life, Dad suddenly took a fall at age 80 that resulted in a downward spiral that rendered this fiercely independent man suddenly dependent.

Caring for Someone You Love, is the story of how this affected both of us. It is a story of love and adjustment and lessons learned, a personal story with broad implications at a time when our older population is larger than ever before in history. With more than 40 million Americans 65 and older, countless sons and daughters will one day find themselves in my position. My father's end of life was an inspiration to me. It is my hope this book will be an inspiration to others.

I am also the author of an earlier book, *Kindness on a Budget*, which illustrates the gifts of being kind daily, both for the giver and the receiver alike. I am an experienced promoter, having discussed *Kindness on a Budget* on numerous radio shows and as a featured guest speaker before various organizations.

My Dad, Jerry Comisar

Born in 1935 and certified brilliant from the get-go, my father enrolled in UCLA at age 16 and went on to earn his PhD in physics with a minor in mathematics. That led to a distinguished career at Aerospace and Mattel, where he was involved in early robotics. He worked mentoring new employees at Selectica, and later in his life taught advanced computer programs at San Jose State University, where he cherished his students.

Always a man of the books, he became a physical fitness enthusiast during the last 15 years of his life, walking and working out daily in the gym and keeping journals of his time and speed on the bike and treadmill.

Divorced twice, Dad had five children in all, each of whom made him proud. He often joked that while he was not good at staying married, he was blessed with children and grandchildren who were both brilliant and kind.

He and I had a special relationship, a complementary one. He was head and I was heart - I was as spiritual in my orientation as he was scientific. That led to many discussions and assigned readings as well as special together moments. We both enjoyed sitting at his desk and watching James Bond and Ex Machina, and we had a shared ritual; we talked to each other on the phone every day between two and two-thirty in the afternoon.

Dr Gerald G. Comisar

1

The Call

One of the hardest phone calls I have ever received took place on a beautiful spring day on April 12, 2015 at 1:24 p.m. I had carefully timed my much needed pedicure to be completed by 2:30, which was the time of my daily phone call with my dad who lived in Northern California. I gratefully arrived at my neighborhood nail salon at 12:15 and carefully turned my cell phone to mute, so I would be forced to "unplug," for the hour and relax. There was a sign above the chair saying "not responsible for cell phone damage," which made me chuckle as I had seen a customer's distress at the phone dropping in the foot bath and could well relate having done similarly in the past!

It was a sunny day and I was feeling so grateful to have my tired feet tended to.

As I left the nail salon at 1:30, I turned on my cell phone and saw that I had eight missed calls from my dad's number! I drove my car around the corner and parked under a tree where there was less shop traffic. I knew immediately that something foreboding was looming and I called his cell crouched in a tight protective ball on the curb. A young man's voice answered my dad's phone and I trembled so badly that I literally felt the earth shaking beneath my freshly painted pink toe nails.

The young man said that he had found my dad seated upright on a curb, injured and confused. He called 9-1-1 and Dad was en route to Stanford Hospital some 30 minutes north in Palo Alto, California via ambulance.

I could hardly breathe, let alone fully begin to process what he was saying. I thanked him profusely for helping my dad and we hung up. In hindsight, I wished I had taken his name and number to properly acknowledge his great care of my dad,

I remembered my 20 plus years of Yogic practice and teachings and told myself literally out loud to breathe deeply. The immensity of the emotions that were running rampant through my body at this point needed my breath to settle down before attempting to drive home.

I began the ten to twelve minute drive home and kept all the windows open, as I still felt a mix between terror to nausea fill my overwhelmed senses. I again self-soothed myself by saying out loud to breathe deeply, and I finally arrived at home.

I truly believe that Angels assisted that short drive as I entered my house shaking uncontrollably with my thoughts racing what to do next. I sat down and called my brother to say Dad had fallen to please call me. I then raced upstairs, two stairs at a time, and took a small suitcase and heaved it on my bed.

There was little rhyme or reason in my packing as all I knew was I needed to get to my dad as fast as possible which was 1,000 miles and a 1-hour plane trip away. I literally tossed in yoga pants, T-shirts, underwear and a toothbrush.

I then called my husband, Peter, who worked an hour away, sobbing and asking him to book me on the very next flight out of John Wayne airport to San Jose, California.

I also forced myself to sit down, at this point with my head between my knees to stave off the pangs of nausea besieging my body. I ate my son's saltine crackers which was what I told him to do on the rare occasion that he was nauseous.

I called my 16-year-old son, Riley, and told him to please come straight home and that I needed a ride to the airport. We had an understanding that if I ever said to come straight home it was an emergency, versus my asking him to clean his room or eat a meal.

I paced on the street corner waiting for him to arrive. My twin brother, Jamie, called and I said I was heading straight to the airport when an unknown number popped up and I quickly got off the phone with him. The call was from a Stanford emergency room neurosurgeon, I froze. He wanted my verbal consent to do a craniotomy to drain the blood surgically from my Dad's brain! I said absolutely not until my brother and I saw our dad and discussed all other options, as I would arrive in 2-3 hours.

My son, Riley, and his (then) girlfriend, Amy, appeared. Amy held my hand for the entire twelve minute car ride, which really was loving and helpful for my jittery nerves. My son asked if I needed him to come into the airport with me and offered to park the car.

Due to my peaking anxieties, I said no as I knew I would be okay and more focused if on my own. When I arrived at the Southwest check-in kiosk, I was still shaking so badly that I couldn't get my credit card in the machine. A true angel of a being, handled my check in and as I explained my situation she told me that she could get me on an earlier flight.

In all my decades of flying, I don't ever recall being escorted to a private "search," area. I explained to the lady that my dad was in a medical emergency, which is why I had booked two flights and thrown my belongings into a suitcase.

As this expressionless young woman checked my items over and over again, a very nice gentleman appeared by my side and said, "Everything will be okay," I joked with him that I was normally a meticulous packer as we both stared at the heap that was my clothes.

I was finally released after 20 minutes and I barely made my 4:10 boarding! I collapsed into my middle seat between two men who would turn out to be my saving GRACE for the flight. Normally when I flew anywhere, I always choose a window seat as I am fortunate to sleep well on airplanes. I also arrive at airports, like my dad, hours early to get a snack, use the restroom, and read a magazine.

The man on my left, a very large framed man, told me that I could lean on him, if I needed to once the flight took off. I thanked him and settled in as best I could, although I was hardly relaxed! The man on my right was immaculate in his attire and I commented on how cheerful his socks were. I told both passengers that I was so very scared to see my dad and what had transpired only hours ago.

Mark on my right called the stewardess and asked for the Wi-Fi code. I watched as he pulled out his lap top and wondered how he could type so quickly. He asked me my name, email, Dad's name, birth date and such. In normal circumstances, I would have paused, yet he seemed determined, He told me he had connections at Stanford and that he wanted to help me and my dad. He shared that six months prior, he had gone through a similar process with his parent and knew both how overwhelming it was and, more importantly, what to do. He sent numerous emails on my dad's behalf to neurosurgeons and hospital staff. If anything, it calmed me down as I had to remain focused to answer his many questions.

Mark told me that my brother and I being my dad's advocates, would give him the best possible chance, just as his advocacy had recently helped his parent.

As the flight landed, which seemed like days not the actual 62 minutes, both passengers walked alongside me as we exited the corridor. I thanked and hugged them both.

I took a minute to gather my wits and straighten my wrinkled jacket and rumpled hair.

As I looked up, I was met by my twin brother, Jamie, whose arms I flew into and sobbed. He took charge of getting us a taxi to the hospital. As we sat in the taxi, my brother said I needed to prepare myself for the worst scenario as Dad had injured his head and brain. Perhaps, I thought he was also telling himself that too.

He had brought with him, my dad's living will that stated clearly and legally what his medical wishes were. We arrived at the huge hospital that spanned many blocks as well as miles. My brother asked the visitors desk lady which room our dad was now in. He was in ICU (intensive care unit) and the five to seven minutes it took to locate him seemed like the walk of doom.

As we entered the ICU ward, the nurses told my brother they were still stabilizing our father and only one person could enter shortly. My brother felt he should see Dad first and then get me, which was a very good decision. As I sat perched against the wall outside his room, I again felt shaky and nauseous from the fear that overtook me.

My brother appeared and said Dad was restrained or, in other words, had his hands tied down for his safety. Brain trauma patients were initially confused and therefore tried to get up as well as remove their tubes and such. I followed my twin brother into the room, not at all emotionally prepared to see my dad as he appeared. I gently approached his left side and sat in a chair that the nurse brought in. I spoke softly to Dad, reassuring him that he would be okay and that Jamie and I were with him.

His eyes were more or less swollen shut and the massive sub dermal bleeding (under his skin) gave him the appearance of a man badly beaten up by a prized fighter.

My brother spoke to Dad and asked him to squeeze his left hand if he understood him, which he did.

All I said over and over again was that we loved him so much and not to worry.

Dad then opened his right eye a small crack and looked my way. Within one hour, neurosurgeons, doctors, nurses and medical students (interns) flanked Dad's sides.

My brother and I immediately wanted to address his brain bleed or sub dermal hematoma. It turns out, I had made the correct "gut instinct," call in saying no to the brain surgery via phone call. My brother who is very composed and commanding despite his 5'7" frame, insisted they do the CAT scan while we were there. The CAT scan confirmed that indeed there was no medical necessity for brain surgery!!!

Seeing our fiercely independent dad tied down like an animal was crushing as well as heartbreaking, and yet we understood it was for his well-being. Each time Dad flailed with his restrained arms, we reassured him that tomorrow he was going to get them removed.

We most certainly understood their place in the initial hours of his injury! As we left the ICU around 11 p.m. we called an Uber driver from the App my son downloaded as neither one of us were in a position to drive under this stress level. We arrived at a nearby hotel that my sister-in-law, Amber, had arranged last minute, as apparently most hotels were sold out as this was a highly populated area or "hub," for business people known as "Silicon Valley."

We both literally collapsed in our beds with pure emotional exhaustion dictating sleep extremely, grateful for the pillow and safe landing pad.

The Lion Roared

On my dad's second day in the ICU, the doctor and his interns appeared. They were telling my brother and me that Dad needed a feeding tube. I couldn't believe that these well-educated Stanford physicians were suggesting such an absurd thing!

I pulled the doctor outside and asked whether he'd even bothered to ask one single question pertaining to my dad's weight or eating habits. He had just been through a traumatizing fall and suffered a brain bleed and the mere suggestion brought me to full center and made me very protective of my dad, now my baby lion cub.

I asked whether he'd happened to notice in the two days that my dad was 5'6". He had been a small framed and slender man and a grazer style eater the last decade of his life. What that meant was that Dad ate small meals throughout the day versus large, typical American style large servings.

He said that he would send a speech specialist in to work with Dad because, due to his brain swelling, he would have difficulty swallowing.

I told my brother and he asked the physician if we could try cream of wheat, pudding and juice, to which he said yes. My brother gently propped Dad up, using the bed controls and I lay a towel on his hospital gown. My brother fed Dad almost the entire cream of wheat, apple juice as well as vanilla pudding without much difficulty.

The speech therapist appeared and explained to us that Dad would most likely not be feeling hunger due to his brain injury, so regular small meals were important.

Dad definitely had some trouble with the juice and she taught Dad, my brother, and me the importance of reminding Dad to clear his throat and pause between bites. Dad had always been a very fast eater, so with each bite, my brother had to wait, which was hard, as Dad seemed eager to eat.

What was terrifying was that if my dad had had no advocate or "Lions" guarding their cub, he would have had a feeding tube, which he clearly did not need at all. He simply needed patience. It seemed evident that the insertion of a feeding tube would have required less time from the nurses.

By day two, we explained very clearly to Dad what had happened to him. He nodded that he understood and yet when we asked him if he knew what happened he said he fell but didn't remember the details. We also told Dad that his hands could be untied if he understood not to try to get up or remove his numerous medical devices. He nodded his head yes. When they untied his slender hands from the bed railings I sighed deeply in gratitude and relief. He had looked like a prisoner.

Over the next few hours, we had to gently remind Dad not to pull his oxygen tubes or IV's out. He needed our reminders for a while and yet I couldn't imagine how invasive all those tubes had to feel. My brother kept quietly reassuring Dad that we would make sure things were handled properly, which seemed to calm him. What was remarkable was that in all his trauma he said he had no pain, aside from his back and only wanted Tylenol, not heavy drugs. This in some way comforted us, as we knew Dad was slowly awakening from his accident. He was never a big pill popper, including over the counter type medications.

I asked the nurse if I could put cool cloths on his eyes, and she said okay. Dad seemed to relax more when these cold washcloths were covering both his eyes and forehead. We quickly learned how to read his oxygen levels and heart rate, and his heart rate became steadier with the hourly cloths. There is something very healing about water and as I covered his swollen eyes, I told him stories about being in a large field of wild poppies with cool, knee high grass. He fell asleep and my brother and I sat near each side watching him appear at peace, grateful for that reprieve from Dad's hourly blood draws and tests.

Day three seemed to be an important day, since the neurologist said it was the first 72 hours that were very important with a brain injury. Dad needed to go for another CAT scan to measure the pressure in his brain, and thankfully it was not higher.

The team decided that Dad could be moved to a sub-acute floor which was essentially one step down from ICU but where the monitoring was a bit more than a regular floor. We were excited about his improvement, albeit small, yet fearful, too, because in ICU the patients were monitored by video and had a shared nursing station between the two adjoining rooms with four patients.

My brother rode in the elevator with Dad as I carried his few belongings to his new floor and room by the stairwell, which was quicker for me. I was now running on pure adrenaline.

Dad's new room was nice as it was better lit than the minimally lit ICU room and had a nice bright window. My brother wrote all of our contact numbers on the white board. Dad was now starting to be able to open his left eye that days before was sealed shut from the blood pooling internally. He actually was more alert but looked worse. He was so bruised along his neck. It was difficult for me to see him so injured. I quickly developed a strategy to only look at his eyes and avoid the horror of his head and neck.

When one is thrust in a traumatizing medical situation, whatever works for you to eliminate the trauma is fine. We all have different coping strategies. I always carry sharpie markers and note cards to write on and I wrote some positive messages and affixed them to the stark white walls.

I wrote:

"This too shall pass. " Hillel
"We love you very much Dad!"
and *"Love heals everything."*

Within a few hours in Dad's new room he was exhausted. The nurses were very kind, and I requested when they spoke about Dad that they addressed him as a person very much alive. What truly shocked me was the way everyone would speak to us as if Dad was a ghost in the room. He told the intern who was speaking at volume ten to please stop shouting at him. Although Dad had hearing aids, he was far from deaf.

I bought a brush in the gift shop and carefully brushed Dad's thick hair, which still had glue in it from the probes monitoring his brain. I also had Dad brush his own teeth, which he did meticulously, so he felt he was still taking part in some of his daily rituals.

My brother and I took turns being in the room. We felt Dad's chances of recovery depended on our presence and fierce advocacy. We told the nurses not to hesitate calling us at night if Dad needed something or was in pain.

As we took the Uber back to the neighborhood hotel, we sat quietly. Seeing our dad in such serious condition as well as being on our A game was beyond tiring. When we got back to our hotel we both brushed our teeth and lay out our clothes in our separate rooms in case we needed to bolt into action. Luckily, we were both able to sleep fairly well, which was a godsend in these intensely hard first few days. We were enormously grateful for Dad's surviving, as well as for a place to rest.

I had no energy to think, so once my head hit the pillow, I was out like a light.

Empathy

Empathy is "the ability to share and understand the feelings of another." An empath, according to the Urban dictionary, is "a person who is capable of feeling the emotions of others, despite that they themselves are not going through the same situation." This defines me accurately, and as a result of navigating my dad's perilous fall almost did me in too.

For those of you who are also empathic or deeply empathic the journey will prove to be harder in many regards.

I have always hated visiting hospitals or cemeteries. It's most certainly not for a lack of caring. The fact is, as soon as I enter a hospital or cemetery, I feel overwhelmed by the feelings that I am picking up from others. I have tried over the years to learn various techniques to protect myself under these delicate circumstances, yet for those of you also deeply empathic there is no "cure all."

In the first days of walking in and out of my dad's ICU (intensive care unit), I wasn't sure I could make it. The man in the bed to the right of Dad was intubated, which means a tube is inserted into the trachea to assist someone unable to breathe on his own. I tried as best as I could not to stare at him. Unfortunately, being in such close proximity, I could hear everything that his physician and family member said, without trying.

They said he had overdosed on vodka and had been in recovery prior to his drinking. His sister said he was 50 and was furious with her brother's negligence with his health.

On day two when my Dad was sound asleep, I could see the man was awake. They had removed his breathing tube and he seemed to be talking to himself. Despite my brain saying, "Don't go over," my heart said, "Yes he needs some supportive words."

I quietly went to his bedside and told him my dad was next to him in pretty bad shape. He said he would pray for my dad which I thanked him for. What was shocking is the day before he looked close to death and 20 years older. Today he appeared strong, healthy and decades younger. I asked him if I could sit down, he said, yes. I know what you are probably thinking, why in God's name with my dad's serious injury, would I sit with a stranger? The answer is that when one is an empath or even deeply empathic you basically can hear and sometimes FEEL another's emotions.

As I sat on a foldable chair, I said that I was so happy he was okay, as yesterday seemed pretty darn scary. He agreed. He told me he had been sober for four years and just "fell off the wagon," in a stressful situation. He further explained he had not tried to kill himself but just to numb his pain. I asked him if he had ever spent time in nature. We spoke about how healing it could be just going up and down hills, much like in life.

We held hands and both prayed, he for my dad and me for his complete healing. Many of you by now will be nodding that you can relate, as hospitals are one of the more challenging arenas for an empath to spend time in.

As I quietly left the ICU the gentleman said, "Ma'am, thank you. I really needed our little talk."

The hard part for those of you caring for an ill or injured loved one is that it can often hurt you as much as it hurts him. In the first two days, I had headaches, puffiness under my eyes and no appetite, much like Dad.

The road of the empathic is a mixed blessing and at times feels somewhat like a curse too. I very much felt the latter the first three weeks of Dad's hospitalization.

One way to achieve relief that helps me is to go outside every few hours. If that is not possible going up and down the stairs can be helpful as "move your body, move your mind."

Taking salt baths helps detoxify some of the energies you may be picking up on.

I was not able to sit in a bath for five weeks. Another option is using aromatherapy to diffuse some of the lingering feelings that do not belong to you. Aromatherapy is a personal choice, yet I used lavender oil for calming. Frankincense was my best friend as it helped me with chronic stress and anxiety. I am not an expert in this field, yet they sure helped me out enormously, thanks to my dear friend, Robin's suggestion.

When Dad was experiencing worry and couldn't articulate it, I felt it. I am sure many of the nurses and doctors thought mistakenly that I was off. I could stand near Dad and feel he was thirsty, cold or irritable without words. I suggest you try what I did if you are an empath and simply say, "Perhaps so and so is cold, anxious or hungry," versus, "I know with certainty that he is!!!"

The next month was equally traumatic, as Dad's skilled nursing home had many more people that I saw daily. One such gentleman, let's call "Stan," would sit all day outside in a dress shirt, tie and sweater. I decided upon "feeling his loneliness and brilliant mind" to arrive earlier to visit with him. I was so grateful that I listened to his silent pleas for interaction. You can easily say that many seniors are alone and therefore lonely, yet this was way more than that.

On our first 30 minute visit, he told me of his stellar career as a professor of literature at Stanford University. He spoke of his wife's passing and having bouts of confusion. We laughed at the five star meals served, as they could easily add five pounds a week, if one were not careful or mindful of his choices.

I heard a man almost 85 who was aware his mind was going and the fact that his only daughter rarely visited. He said she was busy with a professional career as well as teenagers. I shared with him that he was a smart and special man. I visited him every day when I was in town for my dad's rehabilitation.

The day that I had to say goodbye to him, I dreaded it with every fiber of my being. I picked him up a small teddy bear and shyly gave it to him. I explained that I would be flying back home to Southern California and not returning. He and I shared a look that I will never erase from my mind: one of love and sorrow. I hugged him and kissed his cleanly shaven cheek. As tears ran down my face, I told him that I loved him and would never forget him. That is the painful yet beautiful part of being an empathic: you feel more, and it hurts more. Deeply connected individuals experience more emotions, yet suffer too.

When Dad at last moved to Southern California, I literally thought I would have a heart attack. I could feel his discomfort in the car as well as additional frailty. My brother and sister-in-law were amazing, so my brain said "Don't worry," yet my heart and senses said "Please make it here."

I hope this helps you to feel not alone as an empathic or empathic person. Caring is a gift, yet feeling another's pain can be brutal at times for sure. I remember one night, my husband said the house phone was ringing. We have not used our home line in years, as its just for emergency usage. I woke up and immediately could hear and feel that my dad was in distress. I quickly put on my sweat pants and jacket and flew out the door.

As it turned out, Dad had become confused and thought he was living with me. It's expected to have days and even weeks of the "Where-am-I?" state, especially after many moves for a senior loved one.

I decided to lie down on the floor with a blanket and play Dad music to fall asleep too. I also reminded the caregivers and staff that Dad would need reminding in the morning that he was in a new place with my 8:00 a.m. arrival.

What caused me excruciating pain, is I could feel Dad's fear and anxiety. I literally would get a chest pain and shake for no foreseen occurrence.

The good news is that when you are empathic or an empath, you can "feel your way into situations."

What I mean is, being an empathic is a tool too. Dad would tell me one story, his caregivers another and I would simply tune in to what I was feeling, which was almost always, accurate, fortunately!! I was then able to come up with a calm and reasonable game plan, versus an attack or accusatory mode.

Guys, remember, this is a very hard road to travel. No one, including the sensitive empathic, can avoid its pitfalls. The very best words that I can share with you are:

1. Trust your own instincts.
2. Drink tons of fluids.
3. Move your body hourly.
4. Eat well.
5. Share your feelings with a supportive friend, clergy, family member, or spouse.
6. Write your feelings down.

Miracles do Happen

Sometimes you may find, as I did, that good things can come out of very hard situations. When Dad fell, I did not know if he would live. My dad had been divorced a decade and in minimal contact with his ex-wife. Dad also had two children in their late 20"s, whom he deeply loved and cared about. The initial problem on Day One of Dad's ICU (intensive care unit) stay, was that things seemed terrifying. Being a mother of three kids, I knew his children should know what happened. I also had a great appreciation and respect for Dad's ex-wife and sensed calling her was imperative. Because we had not seen one another for a decade or spoken for longer, I had to retrieve her phone number from Dad's cell. I called and said that it was important that she call back regarding Dad, as I just could not leave such a frightening message! Luckily, my call was returned immediately. Helen came the next morning with their son to see Dad. We hugged tightly and I reassured them both that Dad was going to make it. I honestly don't know why I promised that Dad would recover, yet I convinced myself that he would. Having Helen and their son by Dad's side was a tremendous blessing and comfort for Dad as well as me too. Helen's words to Dad were loving and encouraging. In fact, Dad was so happy to see Helen, he was grinning. Helen was a phenomenal support to me and the family during his hospitalization and long rehabilitation. Dad was not easy and was most certainly aware that his way of being had contributed to their marriage ending. Dad had always said "Helen, is an excellent mother. She is also one of the brightest people I know." This is factual. I cannot say enough how the reconnection of Dad's ex-wife helped all of us, especially Dad. Dad would look forward to her weekly visits more than anyone else. He lit up when she visited because of her gentle style and intelligent conversations. Miracles, I believe, occur when we open our hearts to what perhaps our minds say our impossibilities. I am so very grateful for reunifying Dad with his ex-wife, now a dear friend of his and mine.

The Secret Oasis

Those of you who have spent any extended period of time in a large hospital know how exhausting it is just navigating the sheer size of the corridors. I had developed a routine after the first few days, of taking a photo of both the room number and corresponding long hallway. Yes, it was that big of a hospital. On my dad's second week, he unfortunately was in a crisis, as they could not determine the reason for his previous collapse.

My brother, who is a very engaging and sociable guy, was flying home that afternoon as he had meetings to attend. I was planning to sleep on a bench with my sweatshirt jacket as my pillow. I even picked a quiet area that was near my dad's new acute room and near the bathroom.

I quickly learned that it was against hospital policy to spend the night sleeping on one of the hundreds of seats. I was crushed and, more to the point, exhausted.

With my brother enroute to the airport, I felt scared, alone, and sleep deprived. My dad's apartment was simply too far to go in the event of another medical emergency, so I paced the halls thinking about where I could rest when Dad was asleep.

My brother had contacted a lady who ran senior services for VIP clientele who needed their privacy from the public eye. I had no idea what that meant, as I saw us all as basically the same in this heightened stressful situation of caring for our loved ones. I was met by a man who told me to follow him, that my brother's connection had told him where to find me.

I followed him to what looked like offices, and he told me to write down a 4-digit code. He told me that this was a secret room where people could come to eat and nap. I thanked him but said sleep was what I desperately needed if even for a few hours. As we entered this secret oasis, there were drinks, food, snacks and more importantly two couches. He repeated that I should not tell anyone the code, nor the location, as few knew of this even including those employed by the hospital. I slipped off my canvas shoes, took my light weight jacket off and used it as a pillow. I realized it was freezing in the room and as tired as I was I could not begin to locate the air conditioning unit.

I found myself curling up into a little tight ball for warmth. I dozed off. In perhaps 30 or 40 minutes the door opened and the light was turned on and I bolted upright, slightly confused about where I was. A housekeeper told me in limited English "Olympia basura," which I understood was "cleaning the trash." I spoke minimal Spanish, yet showed her I was cold. I also gave her some of the polished fruit and a few of the fancy chocolate bars with cranberries. She hesitated and I pointed to the cameras monitoring the suite and said it was okay.

I went back to my refuge that was the couch and minutes later she quietly appeared with a red woolen Stanford blanket and covered me up. I looked at her through tired teary eyes and said, "Thank you very much."

As I lay on my makeshift bed, not warmed by this caring housekeeper's gift to me, I finally broke down and quietly cried myself to sleep. For those of you who know me, I am a woman who wouldn't hesitate a second offering comfort or help to another. The fact that this dear angel of a lady appeared in my most exhausted and freezing state to warm my body and therefore my spirit was an enormous gift.

As daybreak showed itself through the semi closed blinds, I carefully folded my blanket, drank some tea and took some nuts for my breakfast. I was so grateful to my brother who had met someone who, in turn, allowed me to rest in a room when indeed I was a simple lady caring for her father. I had always been more comfortable with equal treatment for all, so at first being in this fancy suite was not my norm.

As I carefully recalled how to get back to the main hospital, I saw the same lady near the vending machine. This time I said to her, "Thank you from my heart to yours for the warm blanket," and we locked eyes. The gift of kindness is huge and my small gesture of snacks paled in comparison to my aching, tired, cold body having warmth and sleep.

The Roller Coaster

Dealing with the day to day uncertainties about your loved one's health is difficult to manage. There are simply "no guarantees," as we were told again and again. The same is true with life in general, yet when something dramatic occurs, it magnifies it. The notion that we were in control or in charge of anything became a common theme while Dad was so unwell. I faced the same dilemma, many of you will, to want to fix, heal or DO SOMETHING to help Dad get better. Each day, walking towards my dad's hospital room, I would force myself to pause outside his door before entering. This brief five to ten second delay helped a great deal. During that pause, I would breathe in deeply and make a quick prayer for Dad's health. I would also ask that I be blessed with strength to handle what lay before me. I also prayed the nurses, doctors and staff were healthy and positive with Dad.

One morning as I entered Dad's room, they asked me to wait outside. Apparently, he had developed a cut on his foot and they were tending to it. I couldn't imagine how someone as immobile as he, could get injured. Upon reentering the room, the nurse explained that when one is on a blood thinner, the mildest scrapes or bumps can bleed a lot. They were just putting on the proper band aids and ointment to ensure his healing.

Another day, as I returned from lunch, Dad was chipper, talkative and looking great. I asked the nurse what had caused this seemingly improved appearance change that was so marked. She reminded me that as his brain swelling went down, he would possibly have days like this of greater clarity.

The ups and downs were tough to manage. If you are looking for guarantees, do your best to understand that there is no such thing. Once I slowly ingested this hard pill to swallow, I found the ups and downs more manageable. Accept the fact that as much as you'd prefer a smooth path, this one is now guaranteed to be both rocky and windy!!!

An Attitude of Gratitude

Luckily, I had been blessed by leading a yogic lifestyle for some two plus decades, as taught to me by my spiritual teacher, Yogi Bhajan. I was well aware of what a difficult job the staff had in maintaining all the details of both the floor as well as their patients.

My brother was back in Glendale, California. I walked the three miles to the Walgreen's to survey possible treats for the staff as a small measure to say thank you and to acknowledge their support.

I was excited to find a box of chocolate cigars, ironically by "Merci," which means "Thank you" in French. I carefully collected the four small boxes as they were on sale two for $7 and just enough for my plan! As I trekked back to the hospital, I quickly grew tired and rested on a bench.

Back at the main "hub" or nurses and physicians station, I asked if I could use a small portion of the counter. They said yes. I carefully took out the three colored chocolate flavored cigars and carefully spaced out the words THANK YOU!! I had just enough to use the two exclamation marks, and quietly returned to my dad's room with one of each flavor tucked away for my dad who loved to nosh.

I shared with my dad about the chocolate cigar "thank you" and explained to him how important thank you was in our daily encounters. (My dad was a good man, but by no means effusive with his thank-yous and I was hoping to make an impact.

As I popped a chocolate cigar into my dear dad's mouth, I heard him say, "Yummy!"

I went to fill his water pitcher and glanced behind me to see many nurses eagerly eating the chocolate cigars and pointing to the words now quickly fading with each vanishing chocolate. As I carefully poured Dad's water, the nurse's aide appeared to tell us of the tasty treats. I smiled and shared with her, "An attitude of gratitude is the highest yoga," (Yogi Bhajan) She sheepishly asked me if I would write that down. Since wherever I go, I carry sharpie markers and index cards, I wrote it down at once, so not to forget.

Dad and I sat peacefully together as he napped and I rested my head near his side on the bed railing covered with my sweatshirt jacket which I had now worn for weeks! Gratitude filled my heart as I dozed off alongside my daddy.

I Love You

My father and I have been extremely close for the last decade plus. In our phone calls and twice yearly visits, I have always hugged him. I also always have said, "Dad, I love you" before hanging up.

A noticeable shift occurred when my dad fell. I was so "over the moon," grateful that he survived that I said, "I love you," as many times as I could. I didn't say it wanting a response. I was clear that my intention was for Dad in his poor state to KNOW that I loved him, which he did.

My heartfelt invitation to those of you caring for a loved one is to please consider saying "I love you," as often as possible. I realize we all are different and yet we are all the same. Hearing *I love you* is very meaningful as well as healing.

When Dad and I sit in mostly silence at breakfast, I tell him at least two to three times how much I love him. I suppose when one is mindful of her parent's rapid decline, it becomes a priority to speak it.

I also make sure that when Dad tells me he loves me, not to deflect his message but to breathe it in. One day in the not too distant future, I will not hear those words, nor will he. My hope and prayer is that the hundreds of times I expressed my love for Dad will stay with him and me.

I love you are perhaps the three most important words we have to share. I feel being on this harrowing yet sacred journey with my dad has most certainly "awakened" me to their necessity more often than not. I find that even in speaking to friends I say I love you all the time now. This difficult process of facing the reality of your loved one's impending death, is far richer with three words, I do believe: I LOVE YOU

I am sending you so much love as you show up for your beloved family member, friend or spouse.

Code Blue

Aside from getting ""The Call" that my dad fell and seeing him for the first time in ICU, the most difficult and absolutely scariest event occurred on day eight....

The doctors had met with us to let us know on day five that Dad would be going from the hospital directly to a skilled nursing rehab. We had met with their representative at the hospital and were told Dad would have expert physical and occupational therapy five to six days a week, as well as be in a smaller setting to ensure his care. After going over the laborious details with my brother, we had a clear vision and plan for Dad. After hours of talks, we decided that Dad would be transported by a private ambulance company (no sirens), to his new residence some 35 minutes away. My brother would accompany him in the car and I would take an Uber and meet them at the rehabilitation center.

Over the next two days, we collected medical prescriptions as well as doctors' names and contacts, just in case there was a question. The skilled nursing rehab was small in size, which we hoped would help our dad feel safe and more secure. A week in a hospital with interrupted sleep, tests of every imaginable kind, physical therapy and occupational therapy would have exhausted a man half my dad's age, for sure. When we met with the director of new admissions, whom we will call Miss X, she was saying that in four to eight weeks, Dad possibly could be able to return to his apartment with some safety features installed, like a shower rail, toilet riser and such.

My brother handled all of the paperwork and I began to pack up Dad's hospital room in his burgundy suitcase. Dad seemed positive in attitude about the graduation from the hospital, yet understandably unsure.

When the paramedics came to Dad's hospital room to transport him, to say that it was highly emotional would be a gross understatement; it was monumental, as Dad had defied great odds in his progress. The nurses and some of the aides wished Dad good luck and said goodbye.

As they headed out, my brother and I remained strong and upbeat for our dad, despite our own fears. Going down the stairs of Stanford, I raced toward the entry in search of a clear cell signal to call an Uber. Ten minutes later, my driver appeared and I gave the new address.

I asked if I could lie down on the back seat as I desperately needed to shut down for 20 minutes after the weight of the emotions still close below the surface. The Uber driver could not locate the Rehabilitation Center, so I patiently waited till he found it.

We pulled up, and I quickly found Dad in his new room with his bed facing the garden, which my brother had negotiated. It was dinner time and Dad was able to eat and get cozy in his room. The two-person room shared a bathroom with the connecting room so residents could practice and gain their independence over their time there. I was immediately aware of how in some ways this seemed like a huge feat to master as Dad needed help with just about everything now.

I hung up Dad's clothes and put away the items that they had asked us to bring, like tennis shoes, slippers, workout clothes and a bathrobe.

Dad was very tired, so we said our goodnights and told Dad we would see him tomorrow for his first physical therapy session bright and early. We walked around the facility and saw where Dad would begin his more advanced rehabilitation to go home.

We drove to the neighborhood hotel and literally went straight to sleep, both of us sleeping with our phones on.

The next morning, we woke up early. My brother was eating his oatmeal and croissant, yet somehow I felt slightly off and jittery. I told my him I had a strong feeling we needed to get to Dad's right away. He said he would meet me. As I nervously paced in the front of the hotel, I felt fear invade my senses but didn't know why.

The Uber driver pulled up and my brother appeared and we popped in the small vehicle. As we got to the rehab, we walked in and turned the corner in search of the small dining room where residents ate their meals. As we both approached the small door frame, we saw a dark haired girl in her early to mid-20's doing paperwork. A man was seated to her left less than six to eight inches away who appeared grayish/blue. We turned to each other and simultaneously asked, "Is that Dad?!!!!" Within a second we raced towards Dad, who literally looked dead. We barely recognized him.

We tried to get the physical therapist to call 9-1-1. She not only didn't budge; she said he was fine and that the doctor would be there in an hour. We tried rousing Dad but to no avail—touching him, shaking him gently and shouting, "Wake up, Dad." He was a combination of gray and blue and 100% unresponsive. As we screamed for help as loud as we could and got our cells out, a seasoned nurse appeared and yelled in deafening tones, "CODE BLUE, CODE BLUE!!!"

She then raced with our unconscious father, taking expert charge of both him and his wheelchair, and with lightning speed he was in his room, on his bed, with five to six fireman over him.

My brother told me to stay outside, and I literally collapsed to my knees sobbing uncontrollably, clutching the seat of the chair a nurse brought me with my head buried in its plastic center. I kept trying to stand up and go towards my dad's room 15 feet away, but the nurse firmly stood by me until I could breathe again.

My brother motioned for me to enter. He was by Dad's left side (his normal position) and Dad was alert and awake looking pale, yet alive. I leaned on the foreman to steady me as I was shaking uncontrollably and could not move in both shock and fear. The fire captain (let's call him Matt) said "Your Dad had five to seven minutes before he died." He followed it up by saying, "I have seen this here many, many times."

As I drank the juice the nurse told me to drink for shock, Dad said he had no idea what happened and seemed to be tired and a bit dazed, but there was nothing alarming in behavior.

My brother insisted that our dad be taken by ambulance back to Stanford and not the small hospital next door that was affiliated with the rehab center.

Dad had always told us that if anything ever happened to him, "Stanford has the best care."

This time, I took his items and folded them and raced towards Dad and "the team." We had no idea what was to come as the fireman had said it only took oxygen to revive Dad and that he had been, indeed, "Code Blue."

As we headed back the 35 minutes to Stanford, I literally pinched myself to confirm that this was really happening. It seemed like a bad and scary nightmare, but it wasn't.

By the time we got back to Stanford, my dad was put in a holding room in the emergency room. It was loud and very crowded, so only 2 people could enter at a time which in itself was too much due to the tight quarters. As the hours passed, the doctors said they would keep him there overnight on an adjoining wing of the ER that was quieter and where some initial testing could be done.

My brother, who was supposed to fly home that night changed his flight for the next day or so as we took turns checking on our dad.

In some regards, this was a worse scenario Dad was facing. There were no obvious factors such as a fall or high blood pressure which would have warranted him going unconscious.

As we yet again went to a different hotel that my loving sister-in-law found, we collapsed in total disbelief. We both again, put out our clothes for either an emergency, or for the next day and quickly went to sleep. Trauma can wear many different hats, yet what seemed to be a common hat for us was organization and sleep.

The Bunker

During the initial weeks of caring for our dad, my brother and I would take turns going to the bathroom. The bathrooms at Stanford have an arrow how the door locks and yet on many occasions I was greeted by a stranger entering the single stalled bathroom much to my embarrassment!

On one occasion, I carefully put my backpack on the small shelf above the sink and within moments it dropped into the sink where the automatic water soaked it. I carefully wiped it down with the paper towels provided and was relieved to find that the parachute material had kept it more or less damp but unharmed.

I laughed in the bathroom at the absurdity of the water going on motioned by the weight of my backpack, yet despite numerous attempts could not lock the door. When I met my brother for lunch as Dad slept, we laughed about our bathroom experiences.

He had told me that the best bathrooms were called "The Bunkers" They were both air sealed and a good place to relax. Since we had both had intruders enter our bathrooms, I stood outside his men's bathroom to avoid a repeat encounter. The hospital corridor was surprisingly quiet and my brother began to bark in the bathroom. At the exact moment, a security officer asked me if everything was okay! My brother must have heard him as he began to bark very loudly. I burst into uncontrollable laughter and told the perplexed security guard that my twin brother was inside and just joking. He hesitated and then left. I saw him turn around and I waved and gave him the thumbs up sign. At last my brother exited and we laughed at our antics.

When we left the hospital, we were fortunate to be spending many nights at a beautiful hotel that Amber had used her points on for our rest. My brother quickly showed me what he meant by "The Bunker" restroom which was an individual toilet room where I am fairly sure you could scream and no one would hear you! We went to our beautiful rooms to grab tennis shoes and go for an evening walk in downtown Palo Alto. It was amazing how such a silly act of his barking and what followed had truly lifted our spirits.

Codes, Passwords, Keys and Signature Cards are a Must!!

On this difficult journey, I quickly learned that as many details as I knew about my dad, there were plenty facts that remained a mystery in this new puzzle of his life.

When I went to my dad's apartment complex after a few weeks' time, I was able to enter because I had typed in his security access code into my phone. Trust me when I say, these basic facts are needed as you begin to navigate through your loved one's life. I had my dad's apartment and mailbox key, which was critical in getting his mail and other pertinent affairs in order.

As I entered his lobby, I felt the air leave my chest. I had never been to my dad's home without his being present. I was met by the apartment manager who told me she had a large "overflow" box of Dad's mail. I remembered my brother had told me not to say where Dad was, as we didn't know what would be regarding his return home.

I followed Jennifer into her office, She inquired about Dad. She had told me that many residents were concerned if he was okay, as they normally saw him daily in the gym and mail room.

I tried to remain somewhat unemotional, but as I stared down at the large box and saw Dad's calendar from the Audubon Society, which he donated to, tears streamed down my checks. I told the manager who had known Dad for close to 5 years, that he had fallen and was recovering in Stanford Hospital.

She told me she would continue to save his extra mail & parcels in her office. I thanked her and quietly took the two short flights of stairs to his apartment.

Seeing Dad's door, I felt suddenly weak in the knees. I opened his door and immediately placed the heavy box of mail on his small dining room table. The hardest part of all for me, was seeing his empty computer chair with his new floral cushions. I had just replaced his cushions in February as I thought they would offer better back support as well as comfort.

I quickly opened the large patio door as well as screen door. I was so tremendously overcome with sadness and pain in my chest that I forced myself to sit on his empty couch.

The last time, I was there, two months ago, we sat for hours at Dad's computer watching "Patch Adams," a funny Robin Williams classic and his favorite new movie "Ex Machina." As we sat close together watching the movie from his lap top, I recall giving Dad cheese and apples as well as a fresh oatmeal-raisin cookies with water.

Inching my way towards his desk, I felt the room spinning and this time sat at his desk. Seeing all his post it stickers and lists was so emotional. Just weeks before, he'd been an independent man handling almost all aspects of his daily life. As I stared at his computer, I realized he had to have hundreds of emails by then. I made a note to ask his computer log in information and soon learned I didn't even have access to his Wi-Fi as I didn't know his pass code.

Having power of attorney when your parent or loved one falls ill or has an accident helps you only with minimal situations, we found. You are allowed to make medical decisions and sign hospital forms, but that's about it. The key to navigating with ease is to have all of this handy prior to an incident—computer log in names and password codes as well as knowing the carrier and again secret codes.

I lifted the heavy box of mail to the floor, and I started slowly, one bill at a time. Dad had paid some of his bills online. I attempted to call the numbers and explain his situation, in the hope of using my credit card to cover the expenses. No such luck. Even American Express would not allow me to make a payment without my dad's access information and/or speaking to him!!

Signing checks, for your loved ones is also tricky. If you have power of attorney (which my brother did). you can do so with some institutions. I made a significant dent through his bills, but I realized his electricity, phone and rent were my next top priorities. Calling the electric company was successful as I had his bill and ID in front of me. The phone land line was a major ordeal, as they said they would need to speak to Dad. I told them he was incapacitated and I was merely trying to pay his bill.

As I listened to my the numerous answering machine messages—"Your phone bill and public storage bills are past due"—part of me wanted to just wake up from this bad dream.

I asked the public storage to allow me to pay Dad's bill a few months in advance, which they agreed to, if I called from his home phone. It seemed odd, as they obviously knew my female voice was not my dad's!

I cannot stress enough how vital it is to have the details of your parents or loved one's life written down to save you the added strain and time of dealing with bill collectors.

Next, as I surveyed Dad's reminder list on his desk, I needed to call his dentist, eye doctor and pharmacy to cancel and pick up his late prescriptions. Fortunately, I had his wallet with ID which made some of the above doable.

Returning his friends' phone calls was not so easy, as I had limited time and yet wanted to be mindful and appreciative of their genuine concern.

Dad's closest friends all offered their help and support and concern. My dad's book club friends offered to visit him and discuss their latest read.

Dad had instructed me to call his taxi driver and to apologize for missing their agreed upon pick up date, He even said where on the counter I would find his number. It was amazing that he could recall this information and at other times seem so confused.

Seeing his little kitchen with his blue cup in the sink and bagels uneaten and now moldy, was highly emotional too. He was a regimented guy and I could see it in the way his counter was organized.

Keys are very important to have for one's home, access, car, mailboxes and security boxes at banks. You even need a key for public storage these days or you will be denied access.

I began to feel overwhelmed from trying to get a handle on Dad's life, but I knew he would be very upset if bills were paid late. I trudged through the rest of the mail and wrote out numerous checks for Dad to sign as I carefully placed his address labels and a stamp on each bill.

Organization during this time will help you too!

I bought a $2 notebook at CVS and I wrote every bill, check number and contact person's name and number down and dated it for future reference.

I entered my Dad's bedroom, and I knew there was no way I could sleep in there. I found a red blanket and pillow in his closet. I then made a bed for myself on his couch and prayed I would sleep. I had never once slept there, let alone visited without my daddy being home.

The next morning, I realized locating the keys was a must. Knowing my dad as well as I did, I suspected I would find his keys in his sock drawer. Bulls eye!!! The various keys were under the colorful array of socks we had gifted Dad over the years from Pac man socks to preppy argyle.

I decided to walk to his neighborhood Bank of America. The bank manager told me that they would need a signature card from Dad to allow my brother and me to manage his various accounts. Despite my explaining Dad's brain injury and therefore diminished cognitive functioning, she said that was the best they could offer. It struck me as so absurd that we were required to bring Dad in to sign a card in the bank even though he was in the hospital and we wanted to keep his accounts paid and up to date!

If you get your name added to the account, you can avoid these aggravating visits to the bank that yield the same "No, sorry," answer. It's not that the bank didn't want to help me, it's that they legally could not due to their "privacy laws."

I began to walk the mile to Dad's favorite breakfast place "Panera Bread." I felt as if in some way I was attempting to retrace his path on the day of his fall. I tried to get a sense of where he fell as he couldn't remember and the young man who called me had used Dad's phone.

I entered the side door where Dad and I had spent so many special breakfasts together. I felt a wave of dread fill me and I forced myself to order some tea as well as some fresh bagels and cream cheese to bring to Dad. I was immediately met by the hostess who had recognized me and asked, "How is Jerry?"

I told her what happened and she said the bagels and cream cheese was on the house. She came to the side of the register and I hugged her and said thank you. She said they had really missed Dad as he was there practically every day.

Setting up all of one's bills on line may be easier for many of you. Please remember to obtain all the log in information as well as banking data first. If you can't turn on the computer, it makes it much harder, as I soon found out.

I decided to go to the Public Storage. Dad had told me it was in walking distance, which it was. I approached the small office outside their locked gates. The manager whom I had previously spoken to on the phone to pay Dad's bill told me I could not access my Dad's storage without his codes, despite having his key and unit number!

I felt both frustrated and upset and asked for the corporate contact number. I did not know what else to do at this point. I sat on the curb leaving a message explaining I wanted to help my Dad, by going through his unit, but couldn't.

I walked down the street feeling slightly defeated, but I was proud of myself for remaining calm. In heightened times of stress, it is quite normal to have one's nerves frayed.

Heading back to the hospital silently in my Uber driver's shiny blue car, I closed my eyes. I just wanted to sleep and not deal with these extraneous details.

As organized as Dad was and as much as I knew about all the main aspects of his life, this still seemed like an uphill climb.

Please do yourself a huge favor and collect pass codes, key copies and have your name added to bank accounts with your signature card added. In the event of an emergency, illness or accident, you will have way less stress on your already full plate, Dear Ones!

Photo Journal

One thing that may help you greatly on your journey caring for your senior parent or loved one is a photo journal. I took photos of my dad all along his journey sans his ICU nightmare, to visually recant his progress. What is helpful about taking photos is you can look back on the dates and improvements to discuss with the various doctors and therapists.

Early on the doctors were insistent that Dad possibly had a stroke because his face slightly drooped. I knew he had always had that imbalance so pulled up my photographs to substantiate my claim, which it did. I also took photos of Dad sitting down as he had a "computer hunched posture," This also came up with his numerous physical therapists and physicians. They seemed to believe he had other ailments which he did not. In actuality, Dad had a curved spine from numerous hours a day for a decade plus hunched over his beloved computer.

Another super valuable benefit of taking many photos is the memories it will allow for down the road. Some of my most treasured photos of Dad were prior to his accident, sitting in his favorite local cafes as well as at his computer. I also had many photos of him and me at different stages of his recovery that simply show the great love and bond that we shared. Chronicling photos of Dad at Stanford, the skilled nursing and then at his assisted living senior community provided me with great comfort as well as data.

The doctor up North had argued that Dad possibly had a seizure which I knew in my gut was not possible. I spread out the collage of photos until their suspicions were gone as what they were suggesting did not match up at all.

When Dad took was able to use the gym at the skilled nursing facility, I photographed him lifting small arm weights with determination. When Dad took his first steps with his stainless steel walker, I filmed it much as a parent does their child's first steps. When Dad was discouraged with his slow progress, I reminded him how far he had indeed come!

One of my dad's happiest days was when he was walking down the hall with Janet, his incredible physical therapist. He said "Suzanne, I had a Eureka moment. I am walking again!!!" That was Dad's greatest victory to date for sure.

I also brought Dad a framed photo of himself as a jogger in a 5k race with determination on his fixed jaw line. I said "Dad the athlete in you is in your cells." He liked looking at that picture, I believe to boost his hopefulness.

You may consider bringing photos that encourage and inspire your loved one. It helps so much to draw strength and encouragement from photos from the past as well as the present time.

I had brought Dad's old Stanford cap to the nursing home along with the new one I purchased at the hospital gift shop. I have a photo of our two hats on a table side by side that are a marker in part of his and our journey.

One morning when Dad had moved at last to Southern California, I looked down at his shoes. I remembered he had told me how he had researched his new balance shoes for the best support for his walking. I had offered to buy new ones and he said his shoes were comfortable. I replaced the shoe laces with new gray ones and as I carefully tied Dad's laces, he smiled at me. I took a picture of his shoes and socks which were quite poignant as we tracked so many miles together.

Keeping a photo journal is for yourself, at times for your parent, and can be useful with doctors who don't know your loved one's history.

Cell phones today are more than adequate for your photo journal as they imprint the date and location too.

Some of my most special times with my dad are the ones taking him to the lake, the fountain and the yellow umbrellas at the outside mall. I look almost daily at them and I am filled with so much gratitude and love for our shared time spent together.

Breathe

Most of us take our breath for granted. When one is dealing with a new and stressful situation. using breathing techniques can sustain one in turbulent times. I am a yoga student of two plus decades, and I found myself holding my breath during the many traumas I experienced in Dad's journey. Once a friend pointed this out to me, it clicked in. Breathing in deeply and exhaling powerfully is life sustaining as well as balancing. One technique I use when a new health crisis emerges is to inhale positivity and exhale fear. I recommend doing this many times till you feel the energetic shift. Also, I find that sitting on the ground cross legged and breathing in calm, exhaling strain works well too. The beauty of these breathing techniques is that anyone can do them anywhere. When Dad was in the hospital I was shaken and feeling weak. I found the waiting area in his floor and slowed my breathing down. You can breathe in balance and exhale anxiety. This may sound simple because it is, yet when one faces the emotional roller coaster of your loved ones health crisis it is easily forgotten. I also recommend writing in a small index card: REMEMBER TO BREATHE DEEPLY. The deeper the breath, the more space one has in which to traverse these often rocky landscapes. Breath of life is when one focuses on the breath consciously to allow for the clearing out and natural flow of oxygen to the body. Taking small breaks throughout the day to realign with your breath is beneficial and relaxing too! "It's not the life that you lead, but the courage that you bring to it."

~Yogi Bhajan A wise man once told me some 15 years ago, that the deeper the breath, the deeper the life. I believe he was right. My wish for you is that you take care of yourself in this quick and effective manner.

Tears are Necessary

Tears can provide a great deal of relief, I found on this rocky journey. At first, I was able to cry my emotions out freely and naturally. As time passed and I was facing some very scary and unsettling times with my dad, I shut down somewhat. I didn't close down my tear ducts intentionally. I suppose my system needed time to get through and process everything.

Please know that whatever you are experiencing or are feeling is fine. We are all wired differently. Honoring the many layers of sadness, fear, love, grief, and uncertainty is a unique venture. I was shocked by the end of the first month to not be able to cry. I could tear up when I saw my dad in any pain or struggle, yet releasing that heaviness seemed jammed up.

The first few weeks my brother asked me how it was possible to still have tears left, I cried so much. My eyes were so puffy that I needed to use powder to dim down the red hues, as I was mindful not to alarm my dad.

Wherever you are at emotionally, please be loving and accepting of yourself. I found that at times, I wished I could connect to my tears as I felt like the damn would burst from all the pressure.

Sharing with close friends or family the intimate details of care giving helps release some of its strain. One of my dear friends recommended watching a sad movie, which I couldn't muster for months. Trust your own inner compass to guide you as to the timing of the emotional aspect.

When Dad entered the hospital after another fall for the night, I was consumed by fear and grief. I asked Dad if he needed anything and he replied, "Take care of yourself." For some reason, those words lifted the flood gates, and I cried like a baby. I find that what can be helpful is to determine places you feel safe and comfortable to let out a big cry. I felt less self-conscious and secure crying outdoors under a beautiful pine or oak tree. Somehow it made me feel a bit sheltered from the intensity of the feelings beneath the tears.

This may seem obvious, but trust me; it's not! Have plenty of Kleenex in your purse or backpack. During one crying spell, I had to use my nylon yoga jacket to literally blow my nose. While it is funny to me now, I was mortified using my tear laden jacket as my handkerchief.

Even with dear friends, spouses and family around, releasing tears can make many uncomfortable. I began to learn who could hold that sacred space of endless tears without trying to shut them down. It's not being judgmental; people simply do their best given where they are at emotionally too.

I found that, surprisingly, crying in a warm bubble bath with some drops of lavender oil helped enormously too. The inner knowing that we all have gets tested during difficult times. Please do what feels right for you and the rest will be shown in due time.

If you think about how healing water in general is— drinking, bathing, swimming in it— it only would make sense that crying is healing too.

P.S please make sure to stay well hydrated. Releasing pent up emotions and tears can be very dehydrating for some people. I added half a pack of EmergenC to my room temperature water, which helped.

Another soothing element for tears is putting cool cucumbers on your eyelids. Since I did not have any, my son's then-girlfriend ordered me online face masks with various cooling scents. My favorite tissues became the kind that had lotion infused in them. One day, I thought I had bought the same type but had not. When I was blowing my nose in the Uber ride, I soon found out that these had Vicks medicinal vapor rub in them. It was impossible not to burst into laughter because the smell was overwhelming.

I had always carried Kleenex for my dad and supplied his room with his favorite "Puff," brand. How ironic that it took me months to remember to have Kleenex for myself. Taking care of you, even in this small way by having Kleenex, is self-care, therefore self-kindness.

Goals

By week two, it had become very clear that my dad had a very, very long road ahead. As I sat in the hospital Chapel, I got the message that making small goals for Dad and involving him in the process would provide him with hope as well as engage him. As I sat alone in the small yet tranquil chapel, I felt a deep sense of gratitude as well as sorrow rising within. There really was no way to plan for a parent or loved one sustaining a near catastrophic fall, or life altering event.

I took the adjoining stairwell up to Dad's new room. I stopped at the nurses' station to ask If I could take Dad outside in his wheelchair with a nurse's aide.

The charge nurse told me that so long as Dad's heart rate and oxygen levels were stable, we could try and yes, I would need to be accompanied by a nurse.

Dad was sleeping under his red Stanford blanket, which gave him the appearance of a child cloaked in his favorite blanket. I sat close to his right side and just observed his features and the blinking lights that were the constant backdrop of sound in his side of the room.

I pulled out my red sharpie marker and index cards and wrote down some reasonable goals to share with Dad when he woke up.

1. Go into the hospital garden/courtyard one to two times a week.
2. Graduate to a regular diet that was whole foods instead of puree.
3. Have the musician on the floor come in two times a week, which could be arranged through the front desk.
4. Have Dad feed himself at least one meal a day, as we were helping him to ensure his success.

Ten minutes later Dad woke up and I greeted him cheerfully, as I always had during this intense journey. "Hi, Dad, you look so much better today!"

His reply was, "Really, Suzanne?" He straightened himself up a bit. Soon the morning nursing staff arrived to check his vitals and breakfast was brought in. The nurse said that the physical therapist would arrive by 11 and would evaluate Dad to see if, indeed, I could take him with help for a small field trip. Dad's morning tray consisted of apple juice, oatmeal and a yogurt. Due to his recent "code blue," he was having great difficulty swallowing, so the speech therapist wanted him to have all of his food pureed to avoid choking.

I asked Dad if he would be willing to try and feed himself, which would help him to graduate to solid foods, and he said, "Yes." I reminded him with each bite to clear his mouth and swallow before taking the next spoonful, which was frustrating for a speedy eater. Yet he slowed down.

After Dad successfully fed himself his entire breakfast, I went over the date, his birth date, where we were and why. It was part of his daily questionnaire by the doctors to see if he was more cognitively aware, which he was. I joked with him that when the doctor asked who the president was he should say, "Abraham Lincoln," and he smiled.

I brought out my brightly penned index cards and asked Dad if he would like to go outside in the beautiful garden. He said, "Yes."

As we waited for the physical therapist to arrive, I carefully combed my dad's hair and moisturized his dry skin. He still had so many wires and devices attached to him that getting dressed in anything but a gown and hospital pants would not be possible.

Since Dad was a great fan of Stanford, I purchased a burgundy zip up jacket for his first outing. On the left side of the jacket it had STAN and on the right FORD, so when you zipped it up STANFORD was spelled out. I was shocked at the $76 sticker price, yet purchased it to cheer him up. Dad had carried his Stanford book bag with him wherever he ventured out prior to his fall, and I knew he would like it.

The gift shop manager told me that they had some reasonably priced men's pajama bottoms and would save two pairs in size medium when they arrived. I couldn't help but notice how helpful and kind the people I had met these rough two weeks were.

At last, the two physical therapists arrived and I stepped aside to give them room, after respectfully reminding them to please move slowly with Dad, as his greatest fear now was another fall.

The lead therapist spoke very respectfully to him, offering him encouragement with each slight movement. I kept my eyes fixed on the monitor as his field trip required a stable heart rate and oxygenation. After he did 30 minutes of exercise from a chair, they said Dad could go outside for 15 minutes. They carefully put Dad's new Stanford jacket on and I covered his body with the warm blanket.

As we turned the corner, the therapist had me wheel his portable I.V (intravenous fluids) which I found difficult to do smoothly. I asked her if we could switch so I could push Dad to which she said okay.

As we rounded the final corner, the outside doors were in sight, and I breathed in deeply and silently prayed that Dad would remain stable in his new outdoor setting. We parked the wheelchair in part sun, part shade. We sought refuge under a beautiful Pepper tree.

The nurse sat a few feet away on a bench and I kneeled down and held Dad's cold hand. I brought Dad some pudding and apple sauce which I spoon fed him very slowly. He seemed to enjoy the fresh air and outdoor passersby, mostly doctors and nurses on their breaks. I pointed out some of the pretty flowers and trees, much like my dad had done for me as a young child.

Dad dozed off, and I breathed in gratitude and exhaled fear. This was an ongoing battle I faced, in managing the stress of the unknown and also being acutely aware of how deeply grateful and blessed I was to be by my dad's side.

The nurse told me it was time to go back, and we quietly resumed our positions managing Dad carefully through the many hallways.

As we entered Dad's room, he said he enjoyed being outside, yet was very tired. The physical therapists helped Dad back to his bed which was no easy feat. I covered Dad up and told him it was okay to rest.

I left the room to get a bite to eat in the hospital cafeteria which by this time was booming with lunchtime crowds and activity. As I gathered my iced tea and cheese slices and almonds, I went to the outside spot we had just ventured to with peace in my heart. Two goals were met on this new day and I was keenly aware that it was a very positive experience for Dad.

Advocacy and its Many Hats

The definition of an advocate, according to the Merriam-Webster dictionary, is "a person who argues for or supports a cause or policy. A person who works for a cause or group."

That word would take on a whole new meaning and life during the three weeks Dad was in Stanford Hospital, the two subsequent months he was in a skilled nursing facility and the three months that he resided in Assisted Living, a senior community.

In some ways, my brother and I were organized, in that we had Dad's much needed "Living Will," which stated in precise detail his wishes in the event that he was facing death. He had gone over his wishes many times with both my brother and me, so it was pretty much spelled out. What we quickly learned was that it was the in-between spaces that required our strong advocacy of Dad. Some examples are feeding tubes, dietary needs and wishes, secondary opinions and choices requiring medication alternatives. Other important decisions revolved around skilled nursing facilities and how to find the best balance between Dad's wishes and top notch care.

After going through "code blue," at a facility that Stanford had recommended, we became aware of the social services and senior advocacy personnel within the hospital.

My brother and I met with a lady we'll call "Mrs. T," who told us that the best place for skilled nursing was minutes away in Palo Alto, California. We carefully went over our concerns after Dad had just skirted death by minutes.

She said many of the retired Stanford physicians, colleagues and professionals chose this facility for its expert care. We were told by Mrs. T that the waiting list was three months, minimum.

My brother asked her to coordinate our making a visit there with their director. He was now flying back and forth every few weeks, and we both wanted to secure the next place for Dad's rehabilitation now a few weeks away.

My brother also reminded Mrs. T that our father would not be released prematurely, as he had almost died. The daily white board showed his release date days away and my brother insisted it be removed as it created additional anxiety for Dad.

The hospital was so full that as large as it was there were makeshift rooms in some of the hallways, cordoned off by a small curtain. My brother further explained that while we were aware of the maximum capacity, Dad would not be released until they got a handle on his blood clot problem and medication.

My brother made the necessary arrangements to see the place that afternoon.

I asked Mrs. T to please consider asking the hospital for help in getting Dad in there as we he had been through the ringer and we had not filed a claim.

The key to being a parent or loved one's advocate is to be aware of your rights, their wishes, and the details of their insurance plan. Luckily for us, I had saved Dad's physicians names and contact information, and my brother's wife, Amber, retained the details of his medical insurance and supplementary care. I could not begin to imagine how a person navigated through these rough waters without help, information, and support. The fact that there was a senior advocate was unknown to us prior to this experience. It was necessary to keep a notebook with copies of a driver's license or ID card, medical insurance information, names of previous medical doctors, patient's prior history, phone numbers of immediate family, close friends, and housing information, such as manager's names.

The seemingly insurmountable task in caring for one's senior parent or loved one required a very informed advocate as well as the above information. My brother also met one morning with the team of doctors to ask them not to rattle my dad by speaking of his imminent release, when he was far from stable. They concurred.

It takes a lot of energy both emotionally, mentally and physically to handle the myriad of questions and decisions. My best advice to those of you going through this is to find a family member or friend who can walk this rugged terrain with you. Without a shadow of a doubt, without my twin brother's strengths, by my side, I would have collapsed. We learned very quickly what each other's gifts were in handling our dad's health care.

For sure, my brother was best at talking to the administrators, staff, and doctors. He was a force of nature in getting calls back and eliciting their support with our plan.

My strength resided in patience and the spiritual realm, as I used all my experiences as a people person and heart-centered being to unite with the staff.

I have always been uncomfortable around needles and medical apparatus, in part, due to my empathic nature.

Knowing where you need support and again your strengths makes this sticky web less chaotic.

Diagnosis

After a week and a half of intensive tests to try and determine the cause of Dad's "code blue," a brilliant doctor we will name "Dr. L" cracked the code. Dad had spent another night in ICU after his heart rate skyrocketed. My brother who fortunately was, back in town, wore concern on his furrowed brow.

Because the hospital musicians had met my dad on his other sub-acute floor, the staff told the harpist, Pamela, that we requested a visit, if possible, for Dad. I was hoping that the sweet sound of the harp would lower his accelerated heart rate.

When this lovely lady appeared, she sat at first outside the room and played beautiful riveting sounds from her harp. The nurses said it was okay for her to sit on Dad's side of the room, and she quietly relocated her harp, which was on wheels.

As she played, my dad opened his eyes and moved his head towards the soothing, yet ethereal, music. She then approached my dad and told him while touching his hand that she had come to see him as he was her "favorite patient."

I burst into tears at the respectful and kind manner she'd addressed Dad and her exquisite musical ability that had soothed him almost immediately.

After she left, my brother told me that we needed to talk to the doctors in the event that Dad's heart was in further distress, as it had reached an alarming level. Up until this point, they would simply monitor his heart rate which always returned to a normal range in a short time.

As the doctor approached my dad's room, my brother looked at me and said, "Sue, I got this! Go take a break." My brother was far more collected and composed when it came to the very difficult conversations such as "DNR" or "do not resuscitate," which were my dad's wishes and which my brother clarified each life-alarming event.

I was so exhausted and emotionally connected to my dad, that I was grateful he could handle these awful, yet needed, conversations without me.

When I returned, my brother said that Dr. L was moving Dad back to the regular floor and that he believed he had figured out the problem. He said he wanted to do the transfer before his shift was over and would explain to us his findings after.

Again, we sprang into action, packing up Dad's belongings, my brother accompanying Dad to the floor he'd been on previously, while I went directly to the floor to unpack and hang up Dad's belongings and arrange his the hospital table with his items just as he liked it. I also wrote our contact numbers on the white board and highlighted the date as well as our names.

By the time they got Dad all situated in his bed, he was understandably tired and ready for some sleep. I use the term "sleep" loosely as Dad was awakened an average of every 2-3 hours, to monitor his vital signs as well as turn him to avoid bed sores.

The doctor appeared as promised and we went outside the room to discuss his findings. He believed that Dad had a blood clot that was formed in the first week of his hospitalization. He felt strongly that was what caused his "code blue," status. He ruled out stroke, heart issues and other possibilities. He explained that the next morning they world do a CAT scan to support his hypothesis.

We met with Dr L after the results of his CAT scan. Dad, indeed, had several large blood clots in his lungs that were causing the spikes in heart rate as they were close in proximity,

Because Dad was recovering from a Subdural Hematoma, or brain bleed, they could not administer the traditional "clot buster." We asked what Dad's options were and decided to do "the bridge" of Warfarin (blood thinner) extremely slowly and closely monitored. The other option would involve a surgical procedure that we felt, along with the doctors input, was not the best route to take in Dad's precarious state. He told us that if Dad was given too much blood thinner, it could cause his brain to bleed as it was in the early stages of healing.

The brain would need three months to reduce the dramatic swelling.

If Dad was to survive this round, he would be given a small dose of blood thinner in his IV. Once he reached "the therapeutic" levels, Dad would be weaned from the IV medication to an oral regiment, closely monitored, called "the bridge."

This process could take anywhere from a week to three weeks' time, as it would depend on how Dad's body responded to the blood thinner. His only chances of living were to "fight off the beast" that was called a massive blood clot.

We decided to hire a "sitter," to watch Dad from a chair as he slept. He had overcome so many near misses that the last thing we wanted was for him to get up and fall at night with yet another move which was disorienting.

Once the lovely "sitter" named Mary appeared, my brother and I left for a badly needed walk in the fresh air. She spoke in a warm and assured tone as she gently and caringly spoon fed my dad his pudding, which I normally did. She said, "You kids go now and rest and your dad and I will be just fine." I don't know if it was her kind eyes or rich Jamaican accent, but we both just knew Dad was in great care, and said our goodbyes.

My brother was very good at reminding me to eat "real food," as I had subsisted on black tea, almonds, cheese and dark chocolate for close to ten days, sheerly out of fatigue and convenience.

We went to a delicious fish market. I sat staring at my brother. I couldn't believe the MIRACLES we had been blessed to encounter. As I happily ate a beautiful meal, my brother said we should count our blessings.

We simply couldn't fully take in that in a week and a half, our dad had missed 2-3 close brushes with death.

We gathered our weary selves' outdoors and we decided to slowly walk back to our small hotel. Relief set in as the mystery diagnosis was now solved by a brilliant doctor!

Graduation Day for Dad!!!

Three and a half weeks after Dad's fall was a day to celebrate on all fronts!

The fact that he had survived a brain bleed and then a "code blue," was reason enough to be in celebratory mode. We were afraid, too, as to what the next leg of this journey would be like. The nurses and Dr L, in particular, as well as the musicians who had grown fond of Dad were all popping by to wish him and us well. We were all packed up and again, mindful of the last time Dad had been about to graduate and ended up almost dying.

One thing to always be aware of when you are dealing with the many phases of your loved one's health crisis is to take it day to day, as best as you possibly can. I know that sounds a lot easier than it actually is in the reality of a very uncertain situation. What helped me a great deal after the first graduation for Dad from the hospital and subsequent two and a half week "major setback," was to have some outlet that helped me separate from the daily stress. For me, what worked was walking everywhere I possibly could. I also spent time sitting in meditation to strike some semblance of peacefulness. Another tool I used literally every hour, was reminding myself quietly that everything would be okay.

As Dad's new hospital said their final goodbyes, my brother and I accompanied Dad in his private ambulance ride, again sans sirens. My brother sat with Dad in the back and I was able this time to sit up front with the driver. The new skilled nursing home was literally five minutes away and in walking distance from Stanford.

My brother had achieved a true MIRACLE to get Dad in this facility that had a three month waiting list as well as most residents paying strictly cash to reside there. My brother had a way with people that I marveled at. I am much more reserved, yet also warm and caring like my twin brother.

Please note that when you are transitioning to new environments that it can be highly confusing & disorienting for your loved one. We lined the walls with familiar photographs. I additionally placed positive note cards on his bulletin board.

1. Dad, you are so, so LOVED
2. Things are going to get better each day!
3. Laughter is the best medicine.
4. Love heals everything.

I carefully wrote out the date and name of Dad's new temporary home. I also recommend that you clearly place family members' contact information both on the board as well as at the nurse's station.

I hung up Dad's clothes and neatly separated his socks, underwear, short & long sleeve shirts. Workout clothes I lay out on top of his dresser eager for his new physical therapy to begin.

Dad was most certainly confused and yet happy too. He said he could not believe he was out of the hospital which was a very emotional moment to put it mildly. I explained to Dad this was a top notch rehab. What was confusing was that the room actually resembled a hotel or apartment room.

Dad wanted both of his gifted red Stanford blankets on his bed, I imagined for some familiarity. Some of the staff came in and introduced themselves to Dad.

I highly recommend always carrying many pens and one notebook. You, too, may find the numerous people and their titles/ positions and numbers overwhelming, if not jotted down.

As Dad was brought in a late lunch, we sat near him. The food was substantially better than hospital food and Dad said, "I can't believe I am eating real food again,"

Please take a careful look at the rules, regulations and services provided at your family member's residence. The binder was so thick that I literally read it over two hours on the bathroom floor with a high lighter.

In choosing this rehab, it was imperative that we be able to come in at any hour. We also requested, much like at the hospital, to be immediately called in the event that Dad was in distress of any kind. This is a personal family decision to make, yet can prove to be quite important as we found out on many occasions.

As Dad was helped into bedtime clothes, we said our goodbyes. We reminded Dad to please press the button for the nurses and I made him sleep with a small flashlight. It's very important to make sure that your parent or family member has a flashlight as well as the nurses button fastened to their nearby sheets. The length of the cord can easily drop it to the side where it is difficult to retrieve. Small things like a flashlight, offered our dad great comfort.

Nighttime in a rehab can include still many nighttime check ins, therefore sleep disturbances. We got Dad a cozy nighttime eye mask which he really liked. This way if the nurses have to do a quick check of vitals or empty a catheter bag, your family member can stay in a relaxed state. This sleep mask was a true Godsend as Dad quickly equated it with rest.

There are so many emotions associated with a new environment. Routine is a key in making each day have some consistency. We found writing all appointments on one calendar was helpful. Another useful tool is to each day write out the date and year and the appointments scheduled on an index card. I would place this on Dad's table. Having things set up similar to Dad's hospital room table provided him with comfort, he said. When memory is an issue, it helps greatly to have things lined up in a similar fashion to the patient's previous residence. This benefits everyone involved.

I also brought Dad some familiar items from his home like his yellow puff Kleenex box, red water cup and his red stuffed bear, "Teddy."

There is most certainly an adjustment period. Be aware of it, so you don't have false expectations.

Leaving your loved one on a positive note is highly beneficial for his mental state. I always told Dad that tomorrow would be an even better day. I conveyed it with confidence which he in turn could feel. He seemed to like that despite the setbacks that occurred. Please use your discretion on what feels right to say to your parent. I followed my instinct and used the power of positivity to help my father along his long road to recovery.

Adjusting to a New Environment

It is both a time for celebration and a time to pause for adjustment, when a loved one moves to a new senior home. Dad spent nearly a month at Stanford hospital which became his temporary home. He had to adjust to new people, routines as well as the constant "changing of the guards," which occurred both in the early morning and evening shift for the nurses.

It is very important to acclimate yourself with the new environment as quickly as possible.

What I found when Dad had moved to skilled nursing was it was good to know the names of everyone and quickly!!

Here's what helped me:

1. Write down charge nurses names and direct phone lines.
2. Know the names of all the nurses' aides, as they do the bulk of the daily duties.
3. Write down the social workers' direct lines and numbers as these individuals are who you need if there are any issues concerning respectful care.
4. There is usually an "on call doctor," which means if you are not satisfied with the nursing staffs' assessment, they are reachable by phone.
5. Keep your loved one's current records with you for reference. This helps if they are changing medications and dosages, so you have a reference point. (Note: I found on more than 2 occasions, they were giving Dad Tylenol twice a day when he had zero pain.)
6. Leave your phone numbers with the doctor, nurses' aides, physical therapists, social workers and charge nurses: many times I was called after hours.
7. Develop rapport with all the caregivers quickly. These are the people who are the unsung heroes, in my opinion. (*I always

kept a plastic bowl in the room with various candies, chocolates and lollipops for the staff. I affixed a note saying "With gratitude Jerry & family,")

8. Small things like knowing where the fresh water is kept, yogurt and juices as well as extra sheets and towels will help save you precious time as most of even the top facilities are understaffed, as I learned.

Safety is always a priority and when moving a senior to a new place they can become easily disoriented. With Dad, I made sure to remind him daily of where he was and use names of his nurses and caregivers repeatedly. I also wrote down daily scheduling and taped it to his table for backup.

It is vital to know the physicians visiting hours and days.

In private nursing homes, the doctor's often make their own schedules and have limited availability to meet with family members. One thing that worked well for me, was arriving 30 min early and arranging to meet with the staff doctor to review Dad's blood work and issues.

The director of physical and occupational therapy often meets at 8 a.m. to review patients. Please know your rights as an advocate, which includes being present for their discussions.

As now there are strict patient confidentiality laws, you must have copies of your role, which usually entails a signature.

One of the most frustrating aspects of almost all facilities is the weekend staffing! This is a time when physical and occupational therapies are limited. I used these down times to make certain Dad had some exercise and fresh air. Being used to a routine is critical for most people's success in a nursing home setting which includes the weekends.

I also found that I was constantly told and promised one thing regarding Dad's care and then given a list of excuses. The phrase "actions speak louder than words," applies here. Please consider jotting down what you are being told and then following up. I was able to walk into the nursing director's office and speak politely and effectively due to my notes, times and dates. My experience taught me they require details to substantiate your claims.

I recommend you learn the many exits in the facility too. There was a fire alarm that went off twice and due to the deafening ringing, I was able to take Dad to the garden because I had learned the exit doors.

Notifying the staff is always important which is why having the numerous phone numbers with you is so helpful.

The adjustment period in a new place depends on your loved one's health status. For my dad, it took him one to three weeks before he felt used to the new staff and schedule.

I also encourage you to leave a charged cell phone with your parent. Dad called me many times to report different situations. The room phone is difficult to reach and requires an outside dialing code. I hope this helps you too!

The Battle for Independence

Dad was fortunate, even at the age of 80, to be fully continent. He had led a very healthy and active life and stuck to a very specific routine, which, prior to his accident, had served him well. Dad always told me that as much as he enjoyed coffee, he would only, on a very rare occasion, have a decaf, since coffee was a well-known diuretic, He also told me that he tried to drink most of his liquids before 2-3 p.m.

Due to the circumstances of his fall and brain injury, the doctors recommended that the Foley catheter stay in place for the time being to reduce his risk for further falls till he was more physically rehabilitated with his walker. My brother and I agreed after seeking many expert opinions.

During Dad's second month at skilled nursing in Northern California, I made an appointment with his former urologist at a Stanford private practice. Dad had always told me how intelligent his urologist was, so I arranged for a transport van, and off we went. To say that I was nervous would be an understatement. Getting rid of the catheter would give Dad not only more independence, but also a better quality of life, as most assisted living residences for seniors required no catheter.

I brought apple juice and water and carefully timed Dad's drinking them to coincide with his 2 p.m. appointment. It reminded me of being a parent to my young child when he was facing his first day of pre-school sans diaper.

I have always been a very positive person, so I told Dad with conviction that he should not be worried. Today was the day he would have the successful removal of the catheter. Dad then reminded me that his urologist had told him a month earlier, "If you urinated without a problem before, then you will do it again." That seemed to give my dad the extra confidence needed to see his esteemed doctor after a month's time.

As I carefully completed the lengthy paperwork, I glanced at my dad and smiled, giving him a thumbs up.

As we entered the small room, the nurse asked why we were there. I explained that Dad was getting his catheter out. She tersely told me she did not know if that was the case, and with my frail father hanging onto my every word, I firmly, yet politely, told her that indeed he was!!

With the nurse's help, I assisted my dad up the two steps to the table, which was no easy feat. I told her that I would be stepping out for my father's privacy, but she needed to make certain he would not fall off the high table. She assured me she would manage. Five short minutes later, she came out of the room and said, "Sorry, it didn't work."

I looked her in the eyes and told her there was absolutely no way, after everything Dad had endured up to this point that he would be given only five minutes!! I told her to run the water in the sink, the way we had as young parents' decades before to help our kids potty train in the toilet. I told her my father deserved the respect and dignity to be treated patiently, since this outcome would impact his future.

She said okay. With my ear pressed against the door, I heard her turn the faucet on. I sat against the wall quietly praying for his success. In 11 minutes she walked out and said he had been able to urinate the entire amount they had given him.

I hugged her and thanked her for her help.

I returned to Dad, and we waited patiently for the doctor who had many other patients. After 20 minutes, Dad was growing tired. I saw the doctor pass me by and asked him to please not forget the elderly man in room two. He said he wouldn't. When the doctor returned minutes later, he told us that there was no reason to be concerned, as Dad had been able to expel 100% of the fluids. My dad looked relieved and asked the doctor many questions. The doctor was both kind and engaging with my father.

I asked him if he would write down on the form I had brought from the skilled nursing what he'd told us, as I had feared they would be quick to want to put the catheter back in. He asked why, and I explained that the rehab was understaffed, and now they would have to take my dad hourly to the bathroom versus previously waiting three to five hours to change the bag, I felt that due to their obvious staffing deficit, they wouldn't be happy about Dad's victory.

My intuition was accurate. After taking my dad back to his room and making sure he was comfortable in his bed, I brought the charge nurse his paperwork. I told her Dad's great news to which she barked," If we feel that your dad is retaining fluid, we will reinsert the Foley catheter."

To say steam was coming out of the top of my head would be an understatement. I looked her directly in her eyes and said that my dear father deserved dignity and respect, despite their shortage of staff. I made it crystal clear in a firm yet measured tone that I would be meeting with the executive director at 8 a.m. and that my dad would not be in any way compromised.

I returned to my dad's apartment, 35 minutes away, and I quietly cried as I recalled the afternoon's unfolding. Had I not persevered, he would have had to return after those first five minutes with a medical device which greatly limited his freedom.

As I crawled under my blanket on the couch, I kept my phone on, just in case.

The next morning, I arrived extra early and sat outside the executive director's office. As he approached, I said it was urgent that I speak to him. As I quickly surveyed his wall of family photos, I knew I would not leave his office until my dad's care was guaranteed.

He took meticulous notes as I spoke of my concerns about the noticeable lack of staff. I also shared with him that many of the nurses' aides had told me that they were running from room to room without enough help. I made it clear that it seemed to me they were more interested in keeping appearances up, like the art work and crystal ware, than in investing in more nurses. That was when he finally looked up at me and said that I had his word that he would immediately hire extra staff from some floating service of nurses they used.

He also gave me his direct line. I told him that my dad, like his very own parent, deserved to be handled in a respectable manner, which meant that their staffing issues should not affect his having that awful catheter put back. He agreed. I requested that he shake on his word, as I told him in our two months their many promises had not been kept, and that a handshake sealed it. He shook my hand, and I left.

My dad was able with their now increased staff ratio, to spend the next month free from the confines of that rubber tubing and plastic pouch.

While I was deeply grateful for the purpose it served, I couldn't help but think of all the other seniors there who didn't have such a strong and much needed advocate.

As I took Dad along the pretty rose garden, pointing out the hybrid and fragrant buds, I paused and looked up at the huge majestic pine trees and whispered, "Thank you." While it definitely was an adjustment for Dad to now have to go with help many times to the bathroom, he told me he was very relieved.

That night, as I collapsed onto to Dad's cozy couch, I said out loud: " Thank you, dear God. Thank you, dear doctor, and Thank you to the executive director for taking charge of a situation that was long overdue!"

Being a strong and courageous voice for a parent or loved one who is unable to deal with the nuances of his care is paramount for recovery.

Friends

I am so eternally grateful to my small core group of friends who have walked by my side on this journey. Having friends during your loved ones' turmoil makes all the difference, at least for me it has. There have been days that I thought I could not do another thing I was so wiped out emotionally from the strain of Dad's new life. Being able to reach out and ask for what you need is imperative. I would sometimes just ask a friend to simply hold a space of listening. At times, a friend would ask me what is was that I really needed. I found it's okay in this new chapter of your life to not always know what you need. On one such depleting day, a dear friend had arranged for me to sleep at a clean hotel as I was going back and forth. Feeling crisp sheets and a warm shower gave me the added strength that I desperately needed to carry on. People genuinely want to be of help and often don't know how or what to offer. This experience has taught me to slow down long enough to tune in what is needed. It will vary for each of us as we all have different strengths as well as weaknesses. If you are like me a "doer," learning to receive and accept help is new. While at first I believed I could manage everything solo, I was quickly schooled in reaching out for support. If you don't have a close network of friends, there are free services available at hospitals as well as some senior community centers. Please consider putting your pride to the side as taking a hand or an ear or a rest will help to make you your best version possible. I extend to you my love and support.

Trust Your Instincts
Choosing a Skilled Nursing or Assisted Living Residence

When Dad went to the first skilled nursing rehab, I had an uneasy feeling about the director whom we met with. Due to my inexperience and Dad's serious condition, I can now see that I should have trusted my discomfort with the director. After Dad's "code blue," and needing to return to the hospital, I made myself a note saying "Suzie, remember to TRUST your instincts."

As Dad graduated from the hospital to skilled nursing I was very much on "high alert." I noticed that as beautiful as the setting of the new 5-star skilled nursing was, they were visibly understaffed. My main goal was to utilize the excellent physical and occupational therapies offered here. What became shocking was the nurses as well as nurses' aides would often tell me they couldn't do their job adequately due to the ratio of staff to patients. When it became clear that Dad would be able to move to Southern California in the mid-summer, I began my search for his new home. I visited four senior environments that were assisted living as well as skilled nursing in the event that Dad should require more care down the road. I cannot stress enough how crucial it is to go unannounced. The first place I was given a tour by appointment. When I walked into the skilled nursing area ten minutes prior to my appointment, the overwhelming stench overcame me. I was shocked by the sounds, sights and horrible smells. When the manager found me, I said I needed a few minutes and would meet her outside. I literally threw up in the bushes adjacent to the parking lot from the smell alone.

When "Miss V" met me, she assured me this was a top notch place. I forced myself to go on a tour to the neighboring assisted living building that was across the driveway. When I walked in, I saw people who looked sad and a few residents eating in a small dining area. Miss V showed me the residents' common area and it was dimly lit and airless despite the summer month.

I encourage you to trust your instincts, which includes your senses.

When we finished the brief tour, I said thank you, but it was a definite "no" for my dad. As I drove off, I thought that I would never in a million years allow my dad to spend one single day at either location! The mind blowing thing is that this was rated one of the "top senior facilities" and their exorbitant fees were not reflected in anything that I witnessed!

It is important to know your family member's personality, health status, wants and needs before visiting nursing homes or assisted living facilities.

I took a day off before going to the third location and did not announce my arrival. I was scheduled to arrive at 11 and quietly walked in unnoticed at 10. I was immediately aware that the residents in the sitting room and larger living area appeared engaged in activities and seemingly upbeat. As I entered the large residents' dining room, an elderly woman motioned for me. I said I was looking for my dad and that he wasn't with me yet. She insisted I join her for a coffee. As I sat with this incredible lady we will call "Mrs. B," she told me she was 94 and a widow for 12 years. She said she had served in the Royal Air Force in Great Britain. She shared with me that she liked living here, yet sometimes it took a while for staff to arrive at her room. After our visit, I excused myself to meet with the resident's tour director.

I asked many questions:

- ✓ What was the staff ratio for seniors?
- ✓ Could I visit Dad at any time?
- ✓ Was there a plan in the event of a fire or earthquake?
- ✓ Were there lower level rooms with a garden view?
- ✓ Could Dad eat at any time or was mealtime set (as it was at the previous skilled nursing facility)?
- ✓ Was there an emergency pendant for each resident?

After getting all the above questions answered, I was shown sample rooms. Apparently, the first rooms to go are always on the ground level. The director said it would be highly unlikely to get one, as they were all occupied. We went to the various common areas and again, I was delighted to see people reading the newspaper, reading books and talking to each other.

I returned to the director's office and said I wanted to fill out the paperwork.

She said that since I did not know the exact date of Dad's promotion from skilled nursing, it would be hard to do much.

I told her that I knew this was the right place for my Dad. I just sensed it so strongly. She decided to let me complete as much of the lengthy paperwork as possible.

My sister-in-law had found this jewel and I called her from the car. I shared with her both my gratitude as well as my hope that Dad would be able to live here.

Within a few days' time, the director said that a resident was going to move from the garden view room upstairs to larger quarters in two weeks' time. I asked her the room number and said I was 100% certain, my dad would be in that room. I got the floor plans for the room and eagerly began my planning.

I believed in the power of projecting that my dad would live there. I made lists of all the items he would need as well as sketched out where I would put everything. I was so confident in this being the right place that I pre-ordered my dad address labels to be sent to my home.

Within the next three weeks, the contract was signed, deposit paid and I was given access to Dad's "new apartment."

Having a clear vision for the right environment for your loved ones is key. Had I not seen the other three senior places, I would not have known so assuredly that this was a definite YES!! Please make the time to see at least two to three places before making your decision, if possible.

My dad was given an approximate release date of mid-July. Skilled nursing couldn't guarantee it, as he needed to meet certain goals, which he did by a hair.

I spent the next three solid weeks, making everything cozy and cheerful.

I put a bright multicolored fish shower curtain up as well as duct taped a bathroom rug.

I replicated as best as I could Dad's bathroom supplies. I hung cheerful towels and placed his favorite yellow "puff" Kleenex box in 3 locations.

Dad would no longer be cooking or preparing food, but I decided he might feel more as if he was in an apartment with some kitchen items present. I spent hours putting all of his favorite snacks in a variety of sized canisters. My dad was always a great "nosher," or snacker, so it gave me pleasure buying him treats. Dad had told me he liked the big, fat "Snyder pretzels," so I scoured three markets before finding them. I also remember Dad loved Yoplait peach, strawberry & blueberry yogurts and lined his mini fridge with them as well as juice boxes. I did my very best to have Dad's new place warm and inviting, yet not cluttered.

Please do your best to have your loved one's new residence reflect his likes. I was mindful not to do it "my style," but to honor Dad's palette. I also made certain to order a hospital type bed so Dad could go up and down with the controls.

Please note that often these twin XL beds take time to order and deliver.

There are many senior home devices that can be purchased from Amazon as well as specialty stores.

The key for me was safety first and second comfort. My husband located a "lift chair," which is like a lazy boy recliner with the added feature of helping stand you up. Another helpful item, was a table similar to those in hospitals which seniors can adjust to their bed or chair. This table served two purposes in that Dad recognized it and we lined it up exactly like his prior home.

In assisted living there are safety rules, such as that a T.V must be safely secured by a wall mount or brackets. You must also have a seat riser for the toilet that requires drilling in. I highly recommend placing red or yellow caution tape in the shower for the knobs and handles too. Electrical outlets and cords must be carefully tied up as they can be a fall risk for a senior. I put Dad's name on the door with an owl sticker as well as on his mailbox for consistency.

Having an emergency flashlight and whistle is wise too.

I was so very fortunate and blessed to acclimate to Dad's new residence prior to his arrival date. It had 120 rooms so was quite a large multi-story home.

I also got a strong sense of the routines that worked well for others whom I met.

I placed three small plants in Dad's room for some beauty. I even mailed Dad a card so that when he arrived he would have a piece of mail to retrieve. Having a routine when a parent or loved one is moving helps ease the transition.

I also encourage you to speak to family members when searching for a new senior community. I found two visiting daughters, who shared their experiences with me regarding the first few weeks.

I took a risk in furnishing Dad's apartment room and I am glad that I trusted my GUT instinct. I couldn't help but pull my car into the circular drive and imagine Dad here. I also purchased a wheelchair which required assembly. The tennis "cut out" balls for the bottom of the walker is the best $12 you will spend. The tennis balls allow for an easy and slow movement as well as no loud sounds.

I could not believe how fortunate we were to get a ground floor room with a pretty garden room. The compromise was that the room was much smaller, yet the upside was its bright natural light and easy access.

Time

Time is a funny thing. We always think we have an indefinite amount of it, and we don't! I never fully grasped this until my dad's traumatic fall. I always counted on speaking to him daily at 2:30 without any awareness that one day this ritual, too, would pass. Perhaps we don't focus on the precious nature of time until it stares us down with its limitations. I know that for me, I would see my dad at Thanksgiving and the Fourth of July and that was "our special time," aside from our daily phone calls. When you are faced with your senior parent or loved ones illness or injury time takes on a whole new meaning. I found myself starting to bargain with God to please give me more time with my dad. This may occur for you, too, in your situation. As time marched on, I found that I was flying back and forth to spend time with my dad with the awareness that time was of the essence. I began to take our visits in stride and look forward to sitting in my dad's rehabilitation center hours on end. I was wanting and needing more time with my father no matter how it showed itself. What may help you, too, is to slow down and ask yourself "Am I spending the time with my loved one now that is nourishing to my and their soul."? I often explain to my three kids that it is so very important to stay connected with each other and their small extended family. Time has a way of knocking on our door and saying "It's now or never." While I had to pass on many radio and T.V. appearances for my previous book, I am grateful for the time with my dad which has replaced its space. Doing what is right for you is very individual. We are all wired differently in our values and priorities. For me, I have become keenly aware of the clock ticking all too fast. I cherish the hours that I spend each day with my father while remaining unattached to what we actually do together; we simply are just being together. One thing we cannot ever get back is time spent with those we love and cherish. My invitation to you is to sit reflectively and think about who matters to you and spend as much quality time with them as you possibly can. With a full heart it is time for me to go now.

Moving Day!

Dad was finally given his GRADUATION papers from skilled nursing in two weeks' time! He was happy to be moving closer to the family and yet nervous too. We had decided that it would be safer for Dad to be driven the five to six hours to Southern California. Since Dad was on a blood thinner due to his brain bleed, there was a chance he could "drop a clot," from the change in air pressure, which we couldn't risk. We also considered using a sleeper train (my sister-in-law's idea), but soon ruled that out due to the length of travel and bumps.

The plan was in place for my brother and sister-in-law to drive Dad down in their large Ford Flex. My brother drove the car out and Amber flew out a few days later.

We had purchased a lightweight travel wheelchair, walker and special door handle that assisted Dad in getting up. The car was packed to the hilt with his apartment items and some special framed pictures. A cooler was stocked with juice boxes, water and various snacks for the lengthy ride.

The physical therapist had said that it would be safest for Dad to be seated in the front seat. By the time the paperwork was signed, the departure was hours late.

I invite you to consider mapping out gas stations for bathroom breaks and petrol.

It is helpful to also know where there are long stretches of wide open road to plan your toilet breaks accordingly.

Initially, the estimated drive time was five to six hours, but with bathroom breaks and food stops, so Dad could stretch his legs, it turned out to be more like nine hours!!

Please be prepared for all delays, as medication may be a factor as well as needing juice or apple sauce to take it with. It is better to be "over prepared," than "under prepared."

We had a map of all the hospitals just in case of an emergency, which gratefully did not occur.

My husband, Peter and I met Dad, my brother and sister-in-law in the front of his new residence. Being in frequent contact with them, allowed us to be eagerly awaiting his arrival. By the time Dad arrived, he was very, very tired from such a long car trip. Peter helped him out of the chair and I had the room all ready with flowers and some food for Dad waiting.

After another 90 minutes of us all scrambling to bring in boxes and unpack as much as we could, Amber and Jamie left for their home an hour away.

Dad began to look around his room and was happy to see his "secret garden,' picture as well as other familiar photos of family.

Having a familiar setting will help your loved ones with their new move and transition.

Dad ate pasta and cheesecake in his room and got ready for bedtime early.

We stayed with him till he was exhausted and then left.

I cannot stress enough how helpful and supportive it is to have the phone numbers and names of key staff members. This helps alleviate unnecessary worry and therefore provide additional comfort while you are away from your loved one.

I called the front desk an hour later to make sure my dad was okay. Having good communication with the staff will become vital to you and your loved one's transition and overall success.

New Beginnings in Southern California

The Atria would be my Dad's new home the second week of a warm and beautiful summer day in July. It was both a miracle and also a bit scary as Dad's care would not be as intensive as it had been the three months prior.

Quickly, I learned to acclimate Dad to his new senior community that housed both independent and dependent seniors. What was remarkable is that The Atria resembled a pretty apartment complex or "hotel," as my 8-year-old niece said.

At first Dad was concerned about locking his door which I addressed by explaining the halls were monitored carefully by security. The fact was that he was in no danger whatsoever as one could only enter through the front doors which had a sign in desk. He still had his concerns, so I was careful to always have my spare keys with me. I also reflected his concerns, so Dad felt listened to!

The feel of his new place very much felt like a small apartment. As I mentioned in a prior chapter, create as much familiarity as possible. Dad immediately liked his new place and said he saw so many of his favorite belongings which were mostly books and family photographs.

In the beginning, I was careful not to overwhelm my dad with the scope of this large building. I made 1-2 goals a day that usually involved visiting a new living space there. The residents tended to congregate in the front living room where they had a fire place and daily newspapers. The other popular area was a large room where classes were held daily and residents could also relax and read.

The first weeks, Dad was not interested in getting to know any residents or attending classes. He simply was on overwhelm, having just moved from Northern California where he had lived for 25 years.

I invite you to consider researching all the local markets, pharmacies and hospitals. Another useful tip is to find a doctor who does "in-home," visits to lighten your load. I had been ridiculously organized and still had to make numerous changes with doctors and physical therapists.

When one is dealing with changes in housing and independent living, a senior parent needs to still feel a part of the decision making. When I had "Dr. B" come to see Dad, he was friendly. When he showed up three hours late, I let it slide as Dad seemed to like him. When Dad fell and needed help and he called back eight hours later, I let him go. Nice is one thing, being available for calls and prescription refills are another issue. Because Dad was having weekly blood drams for his blood thinner levels, it was critical to find a doctor with good follow through.

Dad immediately liked "the restaurant," which was where the seniors ate all of their meals. The fact that he could order whatever he liked offered him a sense of freedom. The irony is that he eventually would order the very same meals with slight variations daily.

Having a pharmacist who delivers to the family member serves two purposes. One is that they can come quickly if something is required. Secondly, by keeping a credit card on file, it eliminates numerous phone calls.

Forwarding the mail can take one to six weeks, I soon learned. It helps a lot to have a list of the bills you are expecting, to make sure there are no late payments or fees.

I highly recommend checking out which phone carrier works best in your loved one's new home. We needed to have a land line as well as switch cell phone carriers to receive proper reception. Another helpful pointer is forwarding your family member's former phone to the current new number. It is often too time consuming to try and figure out who is calling versus email conversations.

Dad was doing so remarkably the first week that part of me truly believed he was going to fully recover. I was, sadly, very wrong.

When a senior makes such a big move or transition, it is very common for them to fall within the first week. Dad fell just standing at his sink and lost his balance. The caregivers called me immediately and I showed up.

When a senior falls once, he is predisposed for numerous subsequent falls according to the medical research. Dad who had been walking so much more confidently with his walker, was now cringing in pain. Please be mindful of the use of pain medications by checking their interaction with drugs being taken.

Dad's fall set him back both in morale as well as in mobility. Having his "lift chair," which helped him to a standing position was his saving grace. In most skilled nursing and assisted living, a pendant is worn in case of any need. Dad had to adjust to his wrist band as he was used to pressing a nurses' call button. The bathroom also was fitted with a pull cord that sent a message to the caregivers for "help,'

What surprised me was that The Atria had people from all ranges of health issues. A large portion of the aged residents used walkers. a smaller group used wheelchairs, electric and not. Few had canes and a handful required no such devices. It became evident to me at once, that Dad was lucky to be somewhere in the middle of health issues.

Medication is another matter. In Dad's case, I had his morning & evening medications administered to him by a nurse's aide. I simply did not want to risk his forgetting after he had been through the valley of death twice!

It is very costly, to have medications administered and yet if you weigh the expenses of future hospitalizations, if medications are not taken correctly or are forgotten, it becomes a win-win.

I was fortunate to have met a lady named Jane who acted as a "senior advocate," for families. As I was the one overseeing all of my dad's care, I needed some back up support. Companion Care is a service that takes a onetime fee to help ease the mountain of paperwork, questions and resources. I was lucky to have Jane's expertise and caring support during some very challenging times.

Physical therapy was key to my dad's quality of life, in addition to his medication. The first therapist was certainly qualified, and yet Dad didn't like her "military" approach. It is respectful to honor each individual's preferences, if possible.

I had to hire a new physical therapist and Dad was very happy to have been heard and respected in his care. There most definitely is a fine line and balance to achieve in quality care and allowing your loved one to have input.

Each time Dad was moved was a blessing as well as a hurdle. He had many falls which highlighted his fragile state in blinding bright hues. It is vital to pay attention to the cause of the fall, which requires conversations and being calm. In Dad's second fall, I was livid, as he was left alone while his caregiver made his bed. I soon learned that assisted living had its limits too but was a dream compared to the skilled nursing homes I visited.

Being open to the pros and cons will take you time. I would share with you this: "Patience goes along way."

The first time Dad referred to his room as "my apartment," I wept. It was now his new warm and cozy home and for that I was so happy and grateful.

Memories

My memories of Dad are a mixed bunch: some are clear and sweet while others are less pleasant. When I was growing up, my dad was committed to his work as a physicist and mathematician, later an inventor. My parents divorced when I was 12, so that period of time was not easy. I would go every other weekend to my dad's small apartment and accompany him on his plans. Some mornings we would rise at dawn to ready ourselves for his 5 and 10k races which he did bi-monthly. For some reason, I enjoyed those early morning outings, despite the hours of waiting around. First there was registration, then planning where to meet, and then meeting Dad at the finish line, followed by breakfast. I always returned home with a new t-shirt that Dad would give to me, which became my pajamas. When we were small kids, my dad would take my brother and me to the Dorothy Chandler pavilion in downtown Los Angeles. There they would play symphonies on Saturday mornings, which were beautiful. Another happy memory I cherish is going to the bookstores. I was given $10 to buy as many books as I could find. I loved purchasing the Judy Bloom kids series which seemed so comical. Decades ago, there were many bookstores to visit. Since we were limited to one hour a week of television, reading became a source of entertainment and for me a friend. Dad also loved going to Junior's delicatessen where we enjoyed many yummy meals in our youth. Dad recently told me that there were no bagels as tasty as those he used to have at the counter of his favorite deli. Memories for you as you go on this new journey of caring for your senior loved one can provide you with happy glimpses into the past. Yes, it can be difficult to trek down memory lane, as inevitably there will be happy and sad memories; I recommend trying to search your recall to find as many happy ones as you can. I recently pushed Dad in his wheelchair several miles to the last Barnes & Noble bookstore in his neighborhood. My dad was quickly overwhelmed by the volume of people in the store. I took him through some of his favorite aisles, like the travel and psychology sections. He briefly skimmed the books that I placed in his hands. Memories of my dad spending hours on end in such stores came to the surface. My dad asked to go home and tears streamed down my cheeks at the stark contrast of his interest now versus even a year ago. I told Dad that some of my fondest memories were reading the Nancy Drew series that he allowed me to collect on stacks. Another poignant moment came when I took Dad for frozen yogurt. He had always been a great "nosher," or snacker. I wheeled him close to the counter to view all of the many colorful toppings. I sensed at once his confusion and gently offered him a vanilla and chocolate swirl. Sitting in the noonday sun, my dad struggled with his small yogurt. I kneeled down beside him and gently fed him his treat. "Memories are the test of time and all we have from here to our final abode." --Yogi Bhajan I invite you to consider creating as many past and present sweet memories to share with your loved ones.

Kindness Matters

The weeks before Dad moved into his new senior assisted living community, I was there daily. I wanted everything to be as familiar as possible, so I tried my best to replicate things in dad's prior apartment. One day, there was a knock on the door. A friendly woman with her walker introduced herself. Janice had moved in three months before and offered me her help. I gave her a juice box and some cookies with a napkin. She told me that she would be my dad's friend as she too was looking for a friend. I truly bit my cheek as I felt tears welling up quickly. I shared with Janice my appreciation of her kind gesture, I also told her my dad was recovering from a brain injury so was not that talkative or too social. I feared that the scientist, book worm dad I knew would not be as engaging as this lovely lady had hoped.

Every single day, Janice would appear at my dad's room before his arrival. It was touching to say the least. This sweet and vibrant person was my first friend there too which I told her. I asked her questions about her life and quickly learned she was very independent, as well as amazing!

Janice took me to the second floor and pointed out the movie room and beauty salon. The place was quite large, so her generosity gave me an anchoring for Dad's arrival. She recommended that I get Dad involved with the many classes and gym.

Kindness matters so much when you are faced with your new role as caregiver, which I was now. This dear hearted person's daily visits gave me a distraction and support to boot.

Another kind individual I encountered was Jim. He had served as a diver in the US Marines long ago, He told me part of his story, which was incredible. He would go around the perimeter of the large building and pass out flowers.

On a very hard day, as I was sobbing, he gently handed me a red rose and said, "This is for what you are doing for your dad." I hugged him and kissed his cheek. Please, never underestimate what a kind word, gesture, conversation or small gift can do. Kindness is a gift to the giver and receiver alike and therefore can unite and connect us, one kind act at a time. Taking time to really hear what a person is saying or sometimes how they seem is worth your time and efforts, I promise!

The next dear person I met was Jim #2 who sat in the lobby in the same chair daily. He was a retired US military man who kept his cap on his walker. He always said, "Hi, beautiful," to me each day, despite my worn out appearance. We slowly became friends and he would hug me every morning upon going to Dad's room. I must say in all my life, I have never received from a non-family member a warmer or more supportive embrace. When I was gone a few days, he said he missed his hug and I did too!

Daily acts of kindness even in a new environment under great duress uplifts everyone involved. My previous book "*Kindness On A Budget*," shares real life examples like these on the value of being kind daily.

> *"Be kind whenever possible. It's always possible!"*
> ~His Holiness the Dalai Lama

It Takes a Village

Every morning since my dad had his near fatal fall 6 months ago, I usually wake up around 6 a.m. and immediately check my phone, hopeful that there were no calls about Dad during the night.

As I return my cell phone to my bedside table inches away from where I sleep, I always look up towards my high ceiling and fold my hands in prayer pose and say THANK YOU out loud. I find that starting my morning with this ritual gives me peace and comfort, despite what lies ahead....

On this particular early October morning, I was surprised to see it had rained at night and was still lightly drizzling, which isn't so common in Southern California in the early fall.

I got ready, fed Pepper, our six-month-old kitty, poured my 17-year-old breakfast cereal and headed out towards Dad's senior community, five to seven minutes away. Most mornings before meeting my dad for our "breakfast date," at 8:45 a.m., I stopped at the CVS pharmacy to get some items for Dad's room. On this cold and rainy morning, I spotted a small burgundy velvety blanket—perfect size to cover Dad in his wheelchair without excess material getting trapped in his wheels. I also got many boxes of coffee nip caramels which I put in an early Halloween pumpkin on Dad's counter/ledge for his nurses and aides.

What was nice about the caramels was the nurses could grab a few when they visited, which they told me they liked because they didn't need to stop long to enjoy them, "candies on the go."

As I entered Dad's room, I greeted him with a hug and asked him how he felt about an adventure out in the rain. He said, yes.

I carefully packed up the burgundy "Rick Steve's" backpack that he had treasured from his trip to Italy a decade before. Dad had fond memories of his two weeks in Rome & Florence. He often told me about his tour and since he had studied Italian, how he'd been able to order for others in the cafes. His favorite of all, though, was their gelato, which he always told us was the best there was.

I picked a warm sweater and packed a woolen scarf, blanket and snacks for our trek to the lake.

Dad was someone who has always done well with routines, so on this rainy morning, we still stopped at the entry desk so he could pick up an activity sheet. I then wheeled him to a table and put his white napkin in his lap. I always went first to the buffet area to start Dad with cereal with milk and yogurt with fresh fruit. Dad had lost a lot of weight and muscle tone, so proper nutrition was key to his recovery.

As our friendly server took Dad's breakfast down, Dad glanced up at me and I made a heart with my hands and said, "Dad, know what this means?"

He answered, "Yes. I love you too, Suzanne Elise."

My dad was the only person in my life who called me by my legal name, so it was special.

Judy and Nurcian, residents too, who usually sat in the corner window table waved to us. Gene and his wife, Lou, (short for Louis) always stopped at our table and asked Dad how he was. They had moved there together not too long ago for the convenience that the assisted living senior community offered.

Antonio a healthy looking senior with a sparkling smile and Italian accent, also stopped by with his walker and asked Dad if he thought he was getting stronger.

Dad said, "A little."

Antonio shared with us that he was a competitive senior tennis player when he had fallen and needed a steel rod in his right leg. He told Dad that hard work daily was what helped him get stronger and that he would too,

The people who lived in my dad's 120-plus community had varied needs. It was a mix of people in walkers and wheelchairs, sprinkled with a handful who walked with canes. I had only met extremely friendly and kind hearted people who, despite their own challenges, had offered my dad and me encouragement and help.

On Dad's second day living here, a woman named Janice appeared at the door. She told me she lived directly above Dad and would help him get acquainted with his new home as she had lived there for months and also wanted to make a friend. When she said that, a part of my heart ached, as I could feel her beautiful and caring heart. She literally meant what she said and every day when I saw her, my eyes fill with tears for her kindness and her own challenges. She was many years my dad's senior!

After breakfast, Dad and I headed for the front door and told Irwin at the front desk we would be going out for a walk, so the aides wouldn't be concerned about Dad's whereabouts.

I carefully maneuvered Dad's wheelchair, trying my best to avoid the bumps and cracks. We were almost at the end of the driveway when someone called my name. I looked behind me. Dear Judy had walked after us to give us her umbrella.

She was a resident and must have walked quite quickly to have caught up with us!

I hesitated and she said, "You will need it." I thanked her profusely for her thoughtfulness and started towards the Lake. I soon realized that I could not safely push my Dad's wheelchair and hold an umbrella. I stopped and asked Dad if he wanted to continue as it was beginning to rain harder. He said yes. I knelt down and put the umbrella directly over him and told him to use both hands to hold it.

He seemed to be pleased with himself for being able to help in this small way, as mostly everything was now done for Dad which was not easy for him. Just six months earlier he had been 100% independent!

After we had gone about half a mile, I could see Dad's face which appeared very peaceful. That made me so happy.

The rain started coming down heavier, and I asked Dad what he wanted to do.

He said, "Go home," so we carefully, as a team made our way back with my dear dad holding the umbrella as best as he could with me straightening it every ten feet, so he wouldn't get wet.

By the time we returned to his senior community, I was soaking wet, but, much to my delight as I lifted the wet new blanket away, Dad was cozy and warm!!

I saw Judy in the gym and said, thanks again, and that I would leave her umbrella near her room. We locked eyes briefly, and shared a quiet understanding of support and yes, mutual appreciation, too.

By the time Dad got settled and I unpacked the backpack, he was ready for a nap and I was shivering. I said goodbye and kissed Dad's cheek and waited for him to kiss my cheek, which was our daily goodbye.

As I stood at his door, I felt overwhelming love for him and tremendous gratitude for Judy and her umbrella which had helped make our outing possible. I walked out barefoot because my shoes were soaked & squishy I felt emotional about the beauty and love that had been ever present on this day, both from this new community of friends, the staff, and of course, my daddy.

As I started my car and blasted on the heat to dry my wet hair, tears filled my eyes. Every time I left the parking lot, part of me didn't know for certain what tomorrow would bring, so I was moved by our deep bond and also the fragility of his and my new life's journey.

Inspire

I am a person who feels good helping to inspire others. As a young child on the school yard, I would take my brown bagged lunch and sit with other kids who were alone. It simply did not matter to me where they lived or what they looked like. The ability to be kind and inspire others over my almost 52 years has served me well to this point. Being a daughter who is witnessing her father's quick decline takes kindness and inspiring words to help lift Dad's spirits. I am no different than you in that I have tired days as well as cranky moments. The one factor that has allowed me the fortitude of character to endure this very hard path is my kind heart. Today when I was sitting in Dad's breakfast hall, an elderly man motioned for me to come over. I see this gentleman almost daily and call him "\Sir." He said, "Miss, I honor you for the way in which you tend to your father and all of us here. I watch you jump up from your seat many times at breakfast wheeling other residents to their tables who are struggling. I see you carrying extra muffins to the couple who sit beside you. Thank you." I took in what he said and offered thanks. I also shared with him that it was my blessing to help others too. He told me to call him Richard, not Sir and I smiled and returned to Dad. It really doesn't matter where you are personally on your journey. Lifting up others through gestures of kindness is indeed a gift to them and you as well. I got Dad a new short sleeve pale blue shirt as he looks nice in pastels. The caregiver said, " Jerry you are looking so handsome today," to which he smiled and said thank you! Another strategy that may help you too is starting the day with a positive compliment for your parent or loved one. Small gestures can often lift up a senior's mood even if they're not 100% accurate. Telling my dad that he looks great may be a half truth, and yet he feels better hearing it. Also adding encouragement like, "Wow, you really are getting stronger," does more good than harm. This difficult descent of my beloved father's health crisis has accentuated the bright spots in each precious day.

While it is a precarious road, adding some sunlight through words can make all the difference for the one you love. With love to you.

Be a Part of the Solution

In the early days and weeks of my father's fall from grace I was on frayed nerves 24/7. I began to feel like a fierce mother Lion protecting and fighting for her baby cub. As time passed, I was aware that I was so hyper vigilant and sleep deprived that I wasn't as effective as I could be. I encountered so many doctors, nurses, caregivers and social workers that I was overwhelmed by the sheer volume of daily calls and meetings on Dad's behalf. A major shift occurred for me in month four, when I didn't like how I responded to a staff member. I had an "ah ha" moment and heard the words ringing in my ears "It's better to be happy and wrong than right and miserable!" (S.E.A) I turned myself around and started walking into my Dad's senior community with consciousness as to how I would respond to any "incident." What may help you in reading this is to know that when one is under duress, it is normal to be defensive or reactive. The problem with being reactive is that it rarely helps matters. I started writing myself daily notes that said, "Suzie, be a part of the solution," It actually worked well for me. When the head administrator called me into the office to say they would be raising my Dad's rent substantially, I did not react. Instead, what I did was offer suggestions that might help alleviate the extra time the caregivers were spending with Dad. My solution oriented approach helped the caregivers as well as Dad's not having a huge rental increase. I am in no way suggesting that there won't be times you feel angry or reactive. All I am sharing is what worked well for me: being a part of the solution in my every encounter both big and small.

Rite of Passage

As we get older, believing that our parents or loved ones are also aging is often a fleeting thought. I know that when I hit 50 a few years ago, I was still unaware of my parents aging on many levels. For starters, if you are blessed to have a healthy and active parent, the aging factor doesn't always show itself... until it does.

My dad had always been a runner, up until his 60's when his knees could no longer handle the impact. He had been a strict vegetarian for many, many decades. The truth is he was meticulous with his health routines and prideful in regimented health care.

Dad had told me less than a year prior to his fall that what he feared most was losing his ability to think. His next greatest fear was being feeble, which sadly, he now was.

When you are faced with this "midlife" wake up call, it sure helps to tune in to it as best as you can. What I mean by that is there are usually always signs. My dad had started looking slower in his gait and his ability to walk without "shuffling," for some time.

We had discussed the importance of lifting his feet well numerous times. My dad had told me politely that I was starting to sound like a broken record. He was right.

There is another part of this "rite of passage" which involves coming to the awareness that as you are aging, so are your loved ones. Because both of my parents were fiercely independent, it almost served as a distraction from facing their senior status.

Wherever you are at on your journey in years and in health, it helps to do an assessment of where your senior parents are at. As I look back, I can see that there was part of me that still could not fully believe my parents were now "senior citizens," which is quite common. It's not so much denial as it can be that their overall health gives them the appearance of more youthful people.

There are many passages that we experience in our lifetimes. Birth, marriage, parenthood, career, moving and then death meets us all in the end.

I found that at this precarious stage, with my dad teetering between two realms, it was my honor and blessing to serve him, as his daughter.

My dad had always envisioned moving to Southern California and living solo in an apartment near the college. In fact, I had spent some 18 hours making a thick notebook of bus routes, museums, libraries, markets and the best doctors. I even took my youngest son to see apartments that were in walking distance to the gym. Unfortunately, as fate would have it, Dad never moved here under those hopeful terms.

The good news is that with all those hours researching the above requirements for "a move," I was more prepared. By being prepared, I mean that collecting data for your loved ones is no easy feat. It requires calling to see if a doctor or dentist accepts their insurance as well as new patients.

Life can change in an instant. I was fortunate to be able to move up North for an extended period due to my family's support. Not everyone can "drop their life," to act as an advocate and caregiver.

Walking through this sensitive terrain is not easy at all. I was always very close to my dad, so it hurt me to my core watching him suffer. The positive side is that I knew his life and its details well. The rite of passage is in some ways very beautiful, as it mirrors your character and relationship to the person in distress. I feel like the passage for me at almost 52, to be fully committed to my father's care was an immense blessing, but the ups and downs of learning this new phase took time, energy, support and patience. I never realized how patient I was, until I was faced with incredible life altering challenges. Don't be too hard on yourself. Love is a potent force in getting one through these times. Please be patient with yourself and your loved ones as it takes a lot of adjusting to this passage in your and their lives.

I have never done too well with medical sights, sounds, blood or needles. In fact, I often joke with friends that I don't know how I survived childbirth being the sensitive being that I am. The truth is one usually will "rise up," in tough circumstances.

If you have children of your own, please know that they are astute observers as to how you care for your parent. My three kids constantly called to check in on me and always said, "Mama, we will one day do the same great care for you and Daddy."

I pray to God that when my children are faced with this "rite of passage," that they have the support, strength, and compassion to take on this very difficult new role.

The beauty of this marker in time, is that it can also illustrate to you how much stronger and well equipped you are. I, for one, did not know I was capable of so much stress, management and ultimately "service," as I proved to be. Never underestimate the weightiness of this "rite of passage," because your life as you knew it now has entered a new realm. There is beauty, tenderness, sacredness and sorrow as we care for our senior parent or loved one with love, respect, dignity and kindness.

Please tread gently with yourself and those you will inevitably share portions of this passage with. I send you love and strength!

The Bridge

It is often hard to fully understand the dramatic shift that occurs when your loved one changes overnight. In fact, it is like receiving an electrical shock to your system, at best. Half a year into this journey, sometimes I am jarred awake by the current reality that my dad is no longer the father I once knew. Even physically, he no longer appears as he was last Halloween when we enthusiastically passed out candies to his apartment house's many kids. He was standing and erect, now he is frail and in a wheelchair. When you are faced with these new circumstances that are emotionally overwhelming, what may help you is to envision the bridge before you. What I mean by "the bridge" is a walkway that still very much connects you, a bridge that you must cross together in whatever form that may take. For Dad and me that bridge is the two of us venturing forth each new day as a team facing new challenges and physical challenges one step at a time. When my dad had another fall six weeks ago, it appeared that he would die. Blessedly, he did not, and that bridge we crossed required enormous patience and love. Allowing for your loved one to feel a sense of hope and possibility requires being fully present each day. For me, what helps a lot is accepting that I simply do not know what will be. As we cross the bridge together, all I know for sure is that I love my dad very, very much, and that love is enough. Some days as my dad and I cross the bridge he grimaces in pain with each sidewalk crack. Other days, he seems impenetrable from the changes in gradation, and for that I am grateful! The bridge that each of us walks is different. I have come to a place of great patience and serenity about the time my dad and I have left together on this earth plane. The metaphor of the bridge is really about being present and gentle with this delicate balance of life and death. My dad has faced many close calls with death and I was frantic and unglued at all of them. As time goes on, perhaps you, like me, will get to your own bridge with calm and grace. I wish you ease as you walk across The Bridge.

One Day at a Time

One of the biggest adjustments I faced with my dad was the daily changes in his physical and cognitive abilities. At first, I tried as hard as I humanly could to "fix," anything and everything, but to no avail. I did research on the computer to try and find alternative solutions to Dad's health problems. I also got second and third opinions. I was relentless in my pursuit to "save my dad."

I can lovingly offer you this: the sooner you can get to a place where you can accept your loved one's diminished health, the better off you will be. I heard over and over from friends, family and even professionals in the field, "Accept where your Dad's at." Yet I simply could not.

Unfortunately, I wasn't emotionally there yet and spent every fiber of my being trying to build up Dad's health to where he used to be. It took me almost three months till I slowly began to accept this new and super hard reality and it nearly did me in exhaustion-wise.

I began to enter Dad's room intentionally with no more "lists" and "things to do." In fact, I would march in and say "Hi, Dad, you look great," to which Dad would straighten himself up and look pleased. I also stopped my need to control every single aspect of his care, which was very hard as I was Dad's closest child.

Each day, before entering Dads room, I would take a few deep inhales and exhale breaths and tell myself, "Everything is okay." Some days this self-talk helped convince me when my mind said otherwise.

I would invite you to try positive phrases to support yourself in this delicate day to day dance. I also carried a note my brother had left me saying "Best daughter in the world," which gave me strength even when I felt I had none left! The conflict I faced internally was to get to a place where I knew I was doing everything possible to give Dad a quality life, while accepting his current state.

I cannot lie to you; this was so, so hard. I wanted to resurrect my daddy who had been so healthy and vital before but was now a shell of his former self. In hindsight, I wish I had gone to a support group early on. I suggest looking into local churches, temples and hospitals who offer an array of help for the family and main caregiver. It takes an emotional and sometimes physical toll when one is trying to "do it all," which I did.

Each day, Dad would eat his breakfast in the dining hall and then go out. Dad would sit in his wheelchair and I would carefully push him as we ventured out of the community home. At first, we went to just their rose garden, as part of me was scared to be away from the safety of the nurses' aides' help. As I deepened into my acceptance, I found I became more comfortable going on very long walks (many miles) with Dad.

Dad and I were so close, that with my new found confidence and acceptance, he shifted too, perhaps feeling my assuredness. He would choose our route and ask to go further with each passing week. We were able to go to the "yellow umbrellas," which were the tables outside the food court where people gathered. There I would park Dad carefully and return with some new food item. Dad was able to look around and I suppose "feel a normal part," of his day with everyday folks out and about.

I cannot emphasize enough, how acceptance for me, and perhaps for you, too, is a process! I was unable to get to the point of facing "one day at a time," until I fully could accept Dad's current state of being.

A Physician with Compassion

The first month of Dad's move proved to be filled with many "falls from grace." Dad had worked so hard to master his walker and he seemed confident and hopeful. After a series of falls, his world and mine became shaken up, due to the uncertainty of what was causing his repeated falls.

As I shared with you in previous pages, Dad's first "at home," doctor was not a match, as he lacked reasonable follow up and had prescribed narcotics on the phone without seeing him!!

One of the staff members said she had heard great things about a doctor we will call "Dr. S." I scheduled a meeting to have her meet with Dad and see if she was "a fit." This doctor, in her mid to late 50's, had come on her day off, as she received my "plea for help," with Dad. The moment she walked into Dad's room she had a compassionate quality in the way she spoke to him. She joked with Dad that it was her day off and that normally she would be dressed more appropriately, and yet neither Dad nor I cared about her attire!

What stood out instantly was the kind and respectful way she asked Dad questions. Dad's cognitive ability waxed and waned as a result of his brain hemorrhage, so being patient helped. What was remarkable is she told Dad about her interest and studies in physics before she chose medicine and he lit up. Very few people could converse on the intellectual level about the math and physics theorems that they were engaged in.

After nearly two hours, I walked Dr. S outside and thanked her for her help as well as diligence with Dad. She said she got a pretty clear picture of where he was at and enjoyed his brilliant mind.

The difficult part of Dad's journey was his cognitive decline. Dad was 16 years old when he started U.C.L.A. and took great pride in academia, specifically math, physics and science.

I could not have picked a better match for Dad's needs both in professionalism, intelligence and compassionate style. Dr. S wanted me to take Dad to a top cardiologist to rule out heart related issues. She had spent time thinking about his case and did not make quick reactionary decisions.

When Dad had a fall, she came to see him and waited several hours before sending him to the hospital, which was the right call. By the time Dad arrived at the emergency room, Dr. S had already contacted them. Despite its being "after hours," she was in constant contact with the nurses, attending physician as well as me.

When you are face with the trauma of your loved one falling or requiring hospital care, having a doctor you trust is essential.

My dad really respected Dr. S and looked forward to her visits. She offered ideas to keep his mind and body as healthy as possible. At her suggestion, we brought art books with pictures, joined a book club and started showing Dad short news programs.

Please take your time in selecting a doctor that you feel is skilled and has a kind and patient manner. The difference Dr. S made was tremendous. Dad trusted her, I did, and she genuinely seemed to care for Dad's wellbeing.

If you have time, I invite you to interview some physicians first as a kind of "prescreening." method. I was sure the first doctor would be excellent. Reflecting back, it was his secretary who "sold me," on him.

One day when I was leaving Dad's home emotionally drained, I literally bumped into Dr. S. She told me to take care of myself, too, and that I was a devoted and loving daughter. While in my heart I knew this to be true, the rawness of my emotions was palpable.

Spending time finding a physician who resonates well with you and your loved ones is very helpful. I cannot express how this doctor's care and kindness lifted my dad and me during some very unnerving times.

Make Lemonade out of Lemons

One of my grandmother's favorite expressions was to "make lemonade out of lemons." What that meant for her was to create something sweet from something bitter. I often hear my grandma's words echoing in my ears as I approach my dad's room. The focus on seeing or making something positive out of what could be viewed as not is a gift. On one such morning, my dad's caregiver told me Dad wasn't following her instructions in getting out of his chair. Taking a moment to pause instead of reacting is key. I simply reflected her concerns and asked her how I could be of service. Within moments, Dad was getting up easier with one direction at a time instead of two or three. It was a "win-win" for everybody, as she felt heard and successful in helping Dad by limiting her instructions. Dad benefitted by simpler commands. I was at ease as everyone was more relaxed. It is the manner in which one chooses to view such scenarios where the sweetness resides. Months ago, I would have been upset by the caregiver's seeming criticism of Dad. Now I use the tools of pausing and creating a positive result, or "sweet lemonade," to deal with the circumstances. I invite you to try your own style of what may work for you. I am grateful for the shift in being able to see the good in what first appears like a negative situation. Please know that it is par for the course to go through a range of feelings and frustrations. It is difficult to process all of the emotions and changes right away. Please tread lightly on yourself, as that will eventually transfer to how you handle the many others you will inevitably be dealing with. Another helpful pointer is that each new day brings new elements. In embracing the newness of each day, it is my hope that you feel more present to the moment versus the future. Sending you a glass of sweet lemonade...

God Places You Where You are Meant to Be (or A Fall From Grace)

It was Thursday, so I packed a heavier backpack filled with snacks, drinks and ten dollars for a longer walk around town. Entering Dad's room, I always had a mixture of happiness and some anxiety as to how he would be. On this morning, Dad greeted me warmly with, "I'm so glad to see you, Suzanne." I came five to six days a week at the same time, and Dad waited for me. On the rare occasion that I was a few minutes late, I was always surprised that he noticed the few minute difference, as he rarely reflected the time or day.

After kneeling down and kissing his cheek, I busied myself with getting ready.

I did the same thing on most mornings—greeted Dad, laid out fresh pajamas and socks on his bed, opened his blinds and window. Next, I packed up peaches, napkins, V8 juice, pretzels and a few of Dad's mini Hershey bars.

I always took both Dad's prescription and sunglasses along our walks, a charged cell (just in case of emergencies) and a jacket for him.

At 9:05 we were ready to head toward the large dining room or "restaurant," as Dad called it. We stopped by the table for Dad to pick up the schedule of activities for the day.

As I wheeled Dad to a clean table, I sprang into action and prepared his cheerios and plain yogurt with fresh fruit. I always took extra napkins and Dad's decaffeinated tea.

Since Dad was slender, I did my best to make sure he had a balanced and large breakfast. He hadn't eaten eggs in decades but now he always ordered scrambled eggs, a bagel lightly toasted with cream cheese and an orange juice with a straw. Because the tea pots leaked slightly, I always raced to his side to pour it and say "Sir, your tea is ready," which made Dad smile.

When your loved one is requiring extra calories and protein, I invite you to make eating time fun. Using humor and creativity can often help a senior go along with the meals. Dad used to not eat too much, but as soon as I started saying funny stuff, he started eating more. One thing that worked and perhaps may work for you is to decorate the plate. I would put the plain yogurt and surround it with blueberries and make a smile. Another thing was spreading the cream cheese and drawing a heart with the knife. This may seem silly, yet my dad enjoyed these small gestures and in time began to eat more food.

Hydration was a major issue for my dad before and markedly following his fall. Many seniors don't want to drink too much as that means having to urinate more. Being mindful and sensitive to this is important. What may help you too is timing their beverage consumption between outings and appointments to ensure proper hydration as well as being close to a bathroom.

My Dad now was so weak and needed much more time to get to the bathroom, so I would gage his bathroom breaks with fluid intake so he would feel hydrated and also not rushed. Dehydration is a common problem among seniors and can lead to a ton of problems as I found out. Having cups numbered worked well for Dad, as he got frustrated with the repletion to drink. The mathematician in him could relate to numbered cups consumed. Another recommendation is finding a clear water bottle that hold 2 cups of water. I would check off the refills, yet I understand this to be time consuming too,

After breakfast we left the community to head towards the lake. As we pulled up in Dad's wheelchair there was a large sign saying "Warning many bees active here," I quickly saw wasps flying and "bee tailed," out of there. Dad and I found a safe spot a foot from the water's edge. Normally, Dad preferred being near the bench as he worried he could role in. I secured his brakes and sat with my leg literally securing the chair from moving. Once Dad had his small picnic, a large group of ducks fed feet away. He kept clapping his hands, but I assured him they were not going to harm him. Remember, calm and soothing words go a long way and are better than long explanations of ducks' behavior!!

Due to the humidity and 80" weather in November, I asked Dad if he wanted a frozen yogurt. We walked the mile to the stores and Dad enjoyed his cold delight. A woman walked by us and I asked if she could please take a photo. She said she had done the same with her late father and teared up. I teared up seeing her tear up and we soon departed for home. It is precious time to spend with your senior loved one and variety helps break the monotony. Although Dad could not walk or do much, I tried to mix up where we went and what he ate.

As we approached the street just two blocks from Dad's home, I froze. Across the street I could see an older man half sitting and half lying down, separated from his walker. I quickly asked a bicycle rider to please stay with my dad so I could help the man. I darted as fast as I could towards the gentleman. I recognized him at once to be a resident where Dad lived. The community had some very independent seniors, and he was one. I brushed the grass and dirt off him and reassured him. It is hard to keep one's composure at times, when seeing someone injured and down on the ground. Taking deep breaths in and out helps. I was shaken, seeing his head slightly cut with blood. A younger man came to his aide and I asked him to help me sit him up as he appeared only scratched up. I then ran back across the street and got my dad.

I told Dad we needed to help the senior man and hurry back. The nice guy helping me slowly pushed Mr. C. to the residence. I secured Dad and ran for Bryan the director, Bryan went outside and soon the paramedics arrived.

It is very likely when seniors fall, for assisted living or skilled nursing to call the fire department. It was explained to me that they are trained well in assessing the patient and often release them. Note that a patient always has the right to refuse medical treatment. Dad had a fall when he was fine and said no for the hospital which turned out to be a good call on his part. Knowing the parameters of your living situation, can often dictate the plan of action with falls or injuries.

I took Dad back to his room and he said he was very tired. I am sure seeing his daughter race across the street was startling and yet I knew I had to help him.

I checked that Mr. C was okay and left the residence for a cold drink and a cry.

Being able to release your emotions is critical to staying both healthy and balanced. I called a friend and was shaking 20 minutes later recapping what had happened so fast. Truth be told, I was grateful that I was there to help that dear man. My experience has shown me over & over again that "God places us just where we need to be," at the right time.

Be Creative

For half a year I have struggled with getting my dad to stay hydrated and well nourished. The staff has regularly asked me why Dad doesn't eat three meals a day in their lovely dining hall. At first, I was as concerned as they were. Proper fluid intake and diet helps one heal and garner strength. My dad has always been a snacker and minimal eater. He also always drank little to avoid the frequent trips to the bathroom that followed. One day it dawned on me that I needed to get creative in my approach to Dad's nutrition. I took paper and a pen and calculated what a very large breakfast would be, carefully noting each calorie. Since Dad usually stopped his meals by four, dinner was not an option most days. I added it up. With the daily breakfast I served Dad, he was, indeed, fulfilling 85% of his necessary caloric intake!! Next, I purchased every size sealer Tupperware container for his room. I stocked his mini fridge with yogurts, drinks, cheese sticks and bread. When we took our daily walks, I strategically added the remaining 15% of his caloric requirements as well as drinks. Dad was able to put on almost all of his lost weight in three months' time! The good news is, Dad didn't notice the considerably larger breakfast and snacks. I simply made certain to include some of his favorite food items daily and it worked. Looking back at the very many meetings with doctors, nurses, and staff regarding his weight, it was a grand coup. Dad had often said in his early hospitalization he felt "like a stuffed goose." He said he felt like he was constantly being forced to eat. While I understand the doctors were concerned for his health, the approach they took did not work for Dad. Trusting in your own knowingness about your senior parent or loved one is key. Being creative in finding solutions to diet and hydration is possible, I found. We don't all fit into one mold, so while three meals a day works well for some it doesn't for others. May your creative side flow and allow you to create solutions to what you are dealing with.

The Heart of the Matter is Love

There is not a single day that I don't few blessed to be in the position to care for my dad. What drives me to create a beautiful environment and life for my Dad is simply LOVE. I am often asks by different people why don't you hire more help. The answer is this: I AM walking my dad home. What that means for me is that I am not spending time with him out of duty or obligation. I understand that some of you may feel like it is your duty or obligation which is fine. Don't judge yourself if that is the place you are in or compare yourself to others. I derive great inner strength and peace in showing up 5-6 days of the week for my dad. Yes, there have been many consequences of my choice such as stopping a booming book tour and that's okay with me trusting your own inner compass is crucial here. What I mean by that is listen to how you feel and follow that. Each day as I drive to my dad's senior assisted living I am overcome by how grateful I feel. Six months prior, the doctors were not sure if Dad would survive. Each day, I have is a true gift despite its many challenges along the way! I feel I am literally walking Dad home as he edges toward his last chapter. The many miles that he and I have traveled is remarkable. Together we have walked some hundreds of miles, he in the wheelchair, and me learning to properly push it. Please follow your heart as I honestly believe it will help to guide you in what role you choose. I do understand that there are other family members as well As financial decisions that will impact your role. I feel at peace knowing that while my career is on sabbatical my heart is ensconced with LOVE. May love guide you to that very place of knowing that helps make each day easier and a blessing.

It Ain't Easy

It ain't easy in any sense of the imagination to watch your loved one struggling. In fact, it is downright hard and sad too. The hardest part of these last six months have been seeing Dad physically and cognitively diminish before my hazel eyes. My dad for me has always been such a free thinker with strong views and opinions on everything imaginable. When you are faced with this new version of your lives it is quite common to keep looking to the past for any familiar nuances. One thing that has worked for me in accepting this new version of my dad is to notice some of the positive changes in his demeanor. This may prove helpful for you, too, as there are always possibilities of change for the better. One such change that has taken place in my dad is he seems more peaceful and less pensive. He appears more at ease with the staff and residents whom he used to refer to as "the walk-ins." Dad was someone who used to be very particular about whom he liked and engaged with.

When he was living in Northern California, he would get very upset about anyone entering his room he didn't know. In my estimation, he has made peace with the ebb and flow of new care givers as well as nurses who frequent his room. This is a change for the best. Life is about going with the flow, and one cannot always control each detail. It may be helpful, while you face your own journey caring for another to let go of control. For me, letting go of knowing the times and dates of all the appointments has been difficult, yet also liberating. I am I'm some ways like my dad in this regard as I like to know what's happening. Once you enter this phase, the beauty is, you may begin to see shifts in your loved one as well as yourself. It is an illusion at best to believe that we hold the power to control everyone's comings and goings. Trust me, it took me almost half a year to arrive at this stance and it is still new terrain. When you are going through the many ups and downs of bearing witness to your loved one's progress, please be as gentle with yourself as you are with him. Part of this journey has shown me where I am far too harsh on my own self for trying to do it all right. Perfection ain't an easy road to navigate either, so I invite you to consider allowing for imperfections to present themselves. Friends and family continually ask me how I can show up five to six days a week for Dad. My answer is simple: my heart is guiding me to share this most sacred time with Dad in whatever way it shows up. I also warmly encourage you to embrace the notion that whatever you are doing "is enough." I struggled with how hard these last six months have been both emotionally and physically. Some days, I just told myself (self-talk) that I was doing an excellent job to booster my spirits too. May your days be easier as you come to the awareness that it ain't easy, yet it is worthwhile. The one thing that we as humans cannot get back is: TIME I pray for you and I pray for me that we cherish whatever moments we are blessed to share with our family members facing the last stage in their precious lives.

Striking a Balance

When a sudden accident, injury or illness affects your loved one, it is often the case that you are "running on adrenaline," to manage the care. The best advice I can offer you is, make time each day to replenish yourself. I was awful the first five to six months in caring well for myself. I look back now and I can see that I was in "survival mode."

The saying to "put your oxygen mask on first" in the event of plane problems most aptly applies here. It is not enough to have a good support team, if you are not caring for yourself too. It took me seeing a photo of myself to SEE the wear and tear. The problem I faced was that my dad wanted me by his side all the time. He would innocently say, "Are you leaving, Suzanne?" and look crushed. After the fifth or sixth month since his fall, I slowly began to take care of my own self. Self-care looks different to each person. One individual may enjoy a spa day. Another, like me, feels replenished being in nature quietly.

The key to managing your self-care is not to put yourself last as I did. I was so fiercely determined to protect and help my dad that I was blind to my own health.

Once I woke up from the "fog," and began to notice I was depleted, I put together daily "self-care" tasks for myself. What helped me most was to be "off the grid" from phone calls and being still. As this muscle becomes strengthened, you will become clearer on what your needs are. I was not sure at first what I needed as I was still breathing in the "vapor fumes," of my dad's 9-1-1 fall.

On the days that my family could visit Dad, I would look forward to simply being somewhere outdoors. I also replenished myself by walking around the plants and garden centers. Again, each person's needs in self-care will vary. The one common factor though is "time off," to restore one's energy and balance.

I often look back to the first 31 days, when I was every day by my dad's side with inadequate food or self-care. Don't get me wrong; I was received plenty of kind offers to have a break, eat something nutritious, go for a massage and yet I couldn't shift gears.

Often, you may find that the sheer magnitude of "the trauma," can blind side you into "survival mode.' I implore you to find people early on whom you trust who are willing to ensure you get breaks. Having friends and family to speak to can help too. I found that after many months, I was more comfortable sharing with my "inner circle of friends," than attending support groups.

If you are blessed to have friends or family able to just "hold a listening space," that helps too. I learned quickly that I wasn't looking for advice, so much as I was needing an outlet to share this new experience without judgment.

There are also great counselors who specialize in helping during this life-altering event. I was able to find a happy medium of friends, family, counselors and nature to help me feel better.

Anything that becomes an additional "burden" in time and energy will not yield positive results. Options like exercise, gardening, yoga, healthy eating, and being in nature are all possibilities worth looking in to.

My three kids ranging in age from 17-25 also reminded me that if I didn't care for myself, I could not care for my dad! Sometimes, a jarring conversation from your loved ones is the "wake up call," needed towards self-care.

Wheelchairs

Wheelchairs are a form of transportation for a person who is ill or unable to walk. They are also a piece of heavy equipment that most of us block out in our day to day life unless we are in need of them in some capacity.

I remember when my eldest son, Zachary, had a tremendous snowboarding accident on Mammoth mountain. It was a terrifying and dark day in our lives, for our 18-year-old son had broken his back and could not walk. As terror-stricken as I was, I remember fighting back waves of tears as I tried to learn about what type of "temporary," chair he would require.

As many of you know, insurance companies collect their exorbitantly high premiums and yet when it comes time to help, often fall very short monetarily. This was the case as I called to see what best chair would be for my son. They were unable to pay for a lighter weight chair, so we rented a top of the line, more streamlined version.

The traditional metal chair may work for some. In my son's case it was both too wide as well as nearly impossible to lift to put in the trunk of the car.

In addition to purchasing or renting a wheelchair, I learned in the case of Dad that there were different types better suited for his back injury and more supportive.

There are also "transport wheelchairs," that are lightweight yet limited in how far you can walk/push someone. Transport wheelchairs are primarily used for taking a loved one to and from short distances. They are lightweight and fold well. I still needed all of my strength to properly lift and fold it.

Another issue with wheelchairs is that the non-electric models are simply not made for long distances. The wheelchair that I purchased for Dad is four months old and already showing visible wear and tear in addition to a missing screw.

The many miles that I push Dad during the week is wearing hard on his chair. Tightening the screws and keeping it oiled helps a bit.

The problem is that electric wheelchairs are not an option as Dad doesn't have the quick motor skills and cognitive fortitude to drive one.

You might find through your own search that there are benefits to the standard, heavier version as they are what most hospitals and institutions tend to use. It is important to know what your needs are before spending a lot of money. Dad's physical therapist in Northern California strongly advised us to not get an electric one due to the risk factors.

Dad has had many months to make peace with his wheelchair. At first, it is a big adjustment for many as it represents the reality that your loved one is no longer independent. My dad expressed his frustrations about his "darn wheelchair," and I heard him out. It is helpful not to correct one's feelings or experience as it is theirs to have. I remember one day when I was showing Dad the Creek and chimed in that his wheelchair had helped to make this beautiful outing possible as it was clearly too far to walk...He agreed!

That was a big turning point for both Dad and me. He had made peace with his wheelchair and it now represented a new kind of freedom in where we could go. Dad had a very difficult time getting in and out of vehicles due to his injured back and worn knee. The ability to go out for hours in his wheelchair was a bright spot and therefore major turning point in Dad's venturing out and about.

I quickly learned that the fastest and most effective way to clean the wheelchair was to use handiwipes! The wheels collect oil and dirt, so bringing them indoors on carpet creates a mess. What I do is spend ten minutes a few times a week and park the wheelchair on pavement. Then I use the wipes to carefully clean the wheels and foot stands. They are now implementing "clean wheelchair," day at my dad's senior home to combat the greasy carpets.

One of the hardest things in maneuvering another in a wheelchair is the many uneven surfaces. It took me well over a month to realize that going backwards on big bumps helped to eliminate my dad's distress. Also, you will find that it is critical when crossing busy streets to raise your hand to draw the other drivers' attention. People are often in a mad rush and don't always look when making a right turn. Statistically, most pedestrians are struck by cars making a right turn!

I was so shocked at the limited wheelchair accessibility both for my son and Dad. There are sometimes no elevators or wide enough door entries, as Dad and I experienced in the yogurt shop. I had to take off my tennis shoe to keep one door open while I backed in to the other door!!

Please make sure that you stretch and always keep water and a snack with you. I have found that on many an outing with Dad I was without water for myself or a proper snack to recharge.

It will take you time to adjust to pushing your loved one in a wheelchair. It requires using different muscles than the ones used in normal daily life. I found that soaking in Epson salt baths with lavender oil helped release my tight muscles.

There are so many beautiful parks, creeks, lakes and places to go that can be accessible by wheelchair. Good planning helps to avoid the many pitfalls that Dad and I encountered where there were no exits for us. Patience goes along way. Please be kind to yourself:)

Cranes

Since my dad moved to Southern California, he and I have seen a crane or two every time we walk along the creek for miles. The crane always appears at the beginning of our walk, just as we are about to cross over the bridge. At first I thought it was just a coincidence, perhaps a place where cranes eat and relax. After about a month of our trips to the creek, I saw the crane differently. There was no possible way that it was there at varying times and days always in the exact same spot! One morning a man around 60 moved into the bicycle lane for Dad and me to pass with the wheelchair. The road wasn't wide enough for both him and us. We began to see this Asian man many times a week. I asked him if he had noticed the white crane. He said that he had, and that cranes in his Asian culture were a sign for good health, longevity and such. I smiled and slowly repeated it to my dad. Yesterday, as we crossed the bridge, I slightly panicked not seeing "our messenger crane." Turns out it was there but a bit camouflaged. I was somewhat startled by my response, yet immediately knew why! The crane had come to mean health and longevity, so it actually gave me hope. As we walked back, I looked to the far right and saw a group of four cranes literally standing on a circle. I tried to show Dad but they were too far away for him to see. The appearance of so many in the circle formation made me feel at great peace. Perhaps along your journey you may become aware of a repeated animal or insect that seems to give you peace. Animals, insects, birds and plants all have spiritual meaning and therefore significance. I am so deeply grateful for this beautiful and deviate ancient bird crossing our paths. May you be blessed with such beautiful imagery and so potent a messenger.

Peaches

I know what you may be thinking... What do peaches have to do with caring for your senior loved one? I will share with you the gift and blessing peaches have played for Dad and me these last many months. When my dad was in Stanford hospital, for almost a month they fed him applesauce daily as it was easy to swallow. I recall in May my dad saying that he never wanted to eat apple sauce again in his life! I began my search for a new snack that Dad would like that was also easy to swallow as he eats far too fast. Walking up and down the Target food aisles, I saw small individual peaches. I bought four packs and brought them to Dad's small refrigerator. Every morning as I have shared with you, I packed Dad's old burgundy travel backpack for our day out. I packed one small cold peach and a spoon with assorted crackers and treats. From the very first field trip, Dad loved the cold, juicy and sweet tasting peaches. For one, if need be he could eat them at room temperature so fear of spoiling wasn't a concern. There have been many days that my dad is too weak or confused to feed himself his favorite peaches. This saddens me greatly. I simply place a napkin on Dad's jacket and spoon feed him his treat. I can't help but think of the mama bird feeding her babies. I have tried mandarin oranges and mixed fruit cups, yet still Dad's favorite are the peaches. I buy them in bulk and store them in my pantry as Dad's space is too small. Today was the very first day that Dad did not eat his peaches at the lake. It may sound silly, yet it made me aware of his ebbing away from life. We stayed an hour longer at the lake and I could not stop thinking about the peaches and the joy they have brought him. You may be wondering if I like peaches too? Truth is, I associate the sweet peaches with my dad's fall, so I cannot eat them; it's just too emotional a connection for me: peaches and my daddy.

Nature

Nature is all around us. From the moment we step outside, we are surrounded by the sky, the trees, insects and birds. The colors, sights, sounds and scents that are ever present in nature are a beautiful blessing. I understand that not everyone is an "outdoors person," and yet I still would ask you to please be open to looking up a few times a day at the sky, the trees or fragrant flowers.

I have found on my journey, that spending time in nature helps me to feel more in alignment with my body and experiences too. I like to go early in the morning and find a large pine tree and sit beneath its canopy. I suggest taking a bag or towel to sit on as often the trees drop sap. The smell of a pine tree is invigorating as well as soothing, for me.

I have noticed that in the hours I take Dad outdoors in his wheelchair, he appears more relaxed and happy. I sometimes retrieve a small flower or scented pine cone and place it in Dad's hands. He always carefully admires it and smells it too.

There is so much beauty one can absorb by simply spending some time each day in nature. The sounds geese in flight make is unmistakable. Hearing a hummingbird's whistling tweets is uplifting for some. The sight of a rose in bloom releasing its pungent smell is miraculous to experience. No matter where you or your loved one is on their journey, please consider bringing some aspect of nature along with you.

The liquid amber leaves in Dad's neighborhood are quickly dropping their fall leaves. When we go down the pavement, I pause to show Dad their golden and burgundy hues. He seems to like that aspect of nature.

When my dad was middle aged, he took great pride in being a Sierra Club member. They went on various hikes dependent on the skill level of the group. I recall with great affection, the yearly calendars that Dad got for me. They were filled with outstanding colors and scenes from nature's most beautiful places. It is something that we now share in a very organic way.

A white and a gray crane appeared at Dad's nearby creek one morning. The gray crane is not so common. The white crane is so regal and delicate in its long legged structure. The crane represents "longevity," and Dad likes to pause and look at it from the upper bridge.

Dad's community has several gardens residents can walk around. The variety of roses range from white, yellow, red, and purple to hybrids. They smell even without one needing to bend near it. Dad sometimes will tell me of his grandfather, Jacob's love and talent for gardening, how Dad would sit on the stoop and watch his calloused hands tend to the plants and chickens too. He has told me this story many times as it is one of his favorite memories as a young boy.

I truly believe that being in nature helps to bring us back to our own true nature. There is something so exquisite about seeing a blue jay still near a hill standing by to share a song. Another welcome sight are the monarch butterflies that appear on the butterfly bushes. Dad and I had three butterflies surround his chair for at least ten feet of our walk, which was awesome.

Dragon flies are the only "double winged' insect on the planet. Some of them have blue translucent wings. They are messengers of "transformation," in some cultures.

While your loved one, like mine, may be limited in his mobility, being outdoors in nature may offer both of you some tranquility and beauty too: that is my WISH for you!

LOVE is a Potent Balm

One of the beautiful parts of this time with my dad is the great love we have for each other. It is unconditional and not reliant on anything Dad does or says. I show up each day and begin anew with a cheerful disposition and attitude. My only guiding force at this point is to love Dad while he is still here.

I always sit across from him in his small place and lean against the wall. I say 'Dad, know what?" He nods, and then I say, "The deep love we share as daughter and Dad is the most powerful healing one has, so we are lucky!" He always nods and smiles.

Because I have had to adjust and accept Dad's limited verbal conversation, I have come to rely on the nonverbal. At first this was difficult, as he was always the one offering advice, support or ideas. Now he says very little, yet he seems in some ways more peaceful than I have ever noticed in years prior.

Meeting your parent or loved one with love, I truly believe, is your greatest gift to them. It is a feeling and an energy that can be felt with or without words. I show Dad the sign language for "I love you," as well as make a heart with my two hands joined together. He understands this loving gesture and responds well to it.

I understand that people are all different in their expressions of love. All I can offer you is this: Please show up with an open heart and watch what changes in your relationship occur over time. Dad and I had always been great talkers and yet at this last stage of his life, we could spend hours together in silence. The love that he feels and also conveys to me is priceless. Holding a hand or brushing a loved one's hair are also expressions of love.

One cannot overestimate the power of this potent healing balm called love. My dad was never a particularly effusive person and yet he says, "I love you, Suzanne," many times a day. I am certain this sentiment will provide me with deep peace and comfort when he passes away.

I encourage you to be mindful to say as many "I-love-yous as you can to your loved ones. Even if it feels hard at first, it can provide the bridge to deeper healing for yourself and them as well.

I am so fortunate to still have my dad alive after his near fatal fall. Some days when I see him, I get a chest pain having a flash back about all that he and I have been through. The true gift in all of this is for one to cherish and love as much as humanly capable. Time passes all too quickly. Love in words or actions are something so sacred in this limited time in our precious lives.

Strength

There have been many days in the caring for my father that I have questioned my own strength. For starters, this was all new terrain to traverse for me both, in the medical aspect as well as emotional realm. I have been far too hard on myself at times for not knowing what to do or how to feel at the short end of the stick in wanting to do more. The best advice I can offer you is this: be in the present moment. That is all we really have anyways. There is so much involved with the care of a senior loved one. I wish half a year ago, I was told to be gentle with myself! Strength can cover many forms: physical, emotional, mental, and spiritual. While I was always confident in my spiritual nature, I had not been tested to this degree. It took all my decades of yogic training to balance myself out at points when I felt like a sinking vessel out at sea. Whatever practice works best for you spiritually, I encourage you to go there for support. Whether it's prayer or church or yoga, if it helps you, it is worthwhile. Briefly speaking about prayer, I was raised Jewish yet follow a deeply spiritual way of life that is Sikh (a seeker of the truth) and Buddhist (compassion to all). I often spend minutes in my car before seeing Dad asking God to bless him with ease and no pain. I then ask that I am blessed to have the strength to care well for him. Emotional strength varies for each person. I was also tested greatly here as I feel so deeply what another is going through. Being an empathic individual has its blessings and difficulties too. I found this out being a witness to my dad's struggling to eat and then relearn to walk. There were times when I thought I could not bear to see another needle or nurse racing to his bedside. The funny thing is, I surprised myself. I found out that I was stronger than I had given myself credit for. You may find this to be true too. Mental strength can be tricky, as we can often play games in our mind fast forwarding to both the past and the future simultaneously. I found that there were days I was wanting so much for my "old version of Dad," to return or fearing his death that I was tightly wound up in knots. What helped me untangle my worries, was to focus all my attention on what was happening in each day. Yes, the mind can be a beast for us, cultivating scary scenarios or flavoring guilt too. When this tango mentally happens, I would encourage you to simply pause. Taking a few minutes to sit still can work magic in a moment of panic or fear, I found. Lastly, there is physical strength which again will differ for each of you. I prided myself on being active and healthy. I was, however, completely unprepared for the physical toll that pushing my dad in his wheelchair miles a day would have on my body. The expression "place the oxygen mask on yourself first," applies again here. I wrestled with the dilemma of giving my dad freedom outdoors while honoring my fatigued and achy body. Something miraculous occurs when you really stop long enough to hear what your body is saying: it answers you. I began soaking in bath salts every other night and amping up my fluid intake which dramatically helped. At a friend's suggestion, I received monthly acupressure massages to help balance out my sore shoulder and arms. I am not in any way suggesting any of the above comes easy. It is my heartfelt hope and prayer that some of this will help you too. Sending you a big hug.

Dignity

My dad has fallen and he no longer can process, walk or do much for himself. As hard as he tries, with determination and effort, he simply can no longer do much. Once this reality hit me upside the head and hard, I too fell down and cried for days on end. I am not a person, despite my age, who wears much makeup aside from eyeliner. I needed to purchase powder at the drug store to not look frightening to my dear dad. I figured out quickly that although Dad was not able to do much, I would be mindful to keep his dignity intact. What that means is I had to come up with ways to create things that he could do albeit as elementary as they were. In the first day of my "dignity," plan, I wheeled Dad to the lobby and asked him to please help me by picking up the daily schedule. He struggled but was soon able to pick it up after a few attempts. The next day, I had Dad turn the lights off in his room. He hates to "waste electricity." I gently reminded Dad we needed to be mindful to conserve electricity to which he agreed. Another task was to have Dad carry in his lap the cookies we had purchased at the store. He held those like a mother carries her newborn to her bosom. Once a successful exercise was completed, Dad would then start reminding me he needed to do it again—to get the schedule and such!! I also would bring him several choices of jackets and ask him which one he preferred. He seemed to like having a role in something. When we went off for our many hour excursions in the wheelchair, I would always ask Dad which way to go. Sometimes he would point, others answer with a word, and on other days just stare blankly at me. On the days Dad stared blankly, I would kneel next to him and say, "Hey, Dad, would it be okay with you if we went to the creek today?" He would nod or say yes. Despite whatever cognitive impairment or physical limitations one is facing, dignity is important. Trust your own relationship with your loved one to listen to their cues. There is no doubt I could have done everything for Dad, yet to keep him involved in his life, I had to involve him in the process. All human beings deserve dignity and yet it is easy to bypass in a harried life. Dad may need enormous help with mundane daily tasks and necessary living, yet he still is alive and worth the time. Dignity is a gift we give our parents when they can no longer muster it for themselves. The good news is that it actually can yield some small steps in self-pride and therefore dignity too.

Seasons

The changes in seasons are easy to overlook if one lives in Southern California. I have been fortunate to live 50 of my almost 52 years in its beautiful and warm embrace. The beach is 15 minutes from my front door on a bad day's traffic! One thing I became acutely aware of was the weather in Northern, California. The small differences in Palo Alto made me grateful for where I lived a thousand miles south. The first three weeks of Dad's hospitalization, I only had a few T shirts and yoga pants to wear. I also packed one thin athletic jacket and a nice blazer. When I would take breaks in the afternoon I was happy to be in a cool breeze. The change in weather was noticeable to me, as I had rarely worn a jacket.

The magnificence of the mighty oak trees that lined the Stanford grounds gave me great comfort. The strength and breadth of the oak trees canopy is a true beauty in nature. I also became very aware and present to the large geese, deer and majestic cranes I saw regularly. On a particularly grueling day, I glanced out of the window and saw a mother deer with its doe; so gentle and loving. It is easy to take for granted the subtle shifts and presence in nature that one sees in seasons. I would look forward to my 1-2 hour walks each day and allow my glance to soften. I was able to find sustenance and peace surrounding myself in the springtime season unfolding with each new day. Seasons even in their subtle shifts allow us to bathe in their splendor. I invite you to make time in each day to seek refuge in the season. May you be filled with peace as a flower unfolds and its fragrance fills your senses.

Rainbows

Today was a very, very special day for both Dad and me. I had not been able to go yesterday on a long walk due to a pulled muscle. I iced and rested it all day, so as not to miss another day taking Dad out in his wheelchair, which was his freedom.

We began our long walk to the lake and stopped in our usual spot. I always put Dad near to the small cement wall for safety. I also wheeled him backed up to the bench. Dad liked both "our spot," and its view. We went to two other spots before, but Dad said, "Let's go to our favorite spot." This was miraculous in itself, as Dad had been speaking very few words these days let alone complete sentences. I carefully unpacked Dad's little picnic which was more or less the same daily:

1. Peaches
2. Ritz crackers
3. Pretzels
4. Two chocolate (mini) candies
5. V-8 juice with a straw.

We had a special ritual and Dad seemed to prefer familiarity even more these days when his cognitive ability was waning.

Next, I carefully lay napkins over his navy blue sweater as I never wanted Dad to feel embarrassed about spilling his peaches or snacks. Keeping his dignity intact was very important to me. Dad liked it when I popped the small chocolates in his mouth like a Mama bird feeding her young.

I could always see and feel when Dad was relaxed, because he took off his Stanford cap and passed me his sunglasses. This always made me sigh a breath of relief as some days Dad's face appeared strained.

I sat to the left of Dad's wheelchair on the ground as I knew he liked me close by. I said "Hey, Dad, isn't this so tranquil? to which he replied, "Sure is, Suzanne."

After around 40 minutes, I looked at the spouting fountain and a rainbow appeared through its center. The sky was clear blue without a cloud in sight. At first I thought it was my eyes playing tricks on me. I said "Dad, please look at our fountain and tell me what you see."

After a five to ten second pause, which was usual these days for Dad, he said, "I see a rainbow, Wow!"

The other amazing thing about our special lake spot was in all these four months, we were lucky that our little corner and bench were always vacant.

I told Dad that I intended to call the City office to see if he and I could put up a placard on the bench saying "Dad & Suzie's favorite place." He smiled and nodded.

Every rainbow has seven colors: red, orange. yellow, green, blue, Indigo & violet.

According to the Bible, it is believed that a "rainbow is a sign from the Almighty that we are not forgotten".

The seven colors of the rainbow represent:

1. Red-signifies passion, vitality, enthusiasm and enthusiasm.
2. Orange - a dynamic color, represents creativity, practicality, playfulness, as well as equilibrium and control.
3. Yellow - the color of the sunshine itself, represents clarity of thought, wisdom, orderliness, and energy.
4. Green - denotes fertility, balance, growth, health, and wealth.
5. Blue - associated with the sky and oceans and makes us think of the unknown, spirituality and divinity.
6. Indigo - thought to be both sedating as well as used for self-awareness and enhancement of Intuition.
7. Violet - considered the highest element of spirituality, associated with igniting ones imagination, with sorrow in its darker tones. Deeper shades of violet or purple denote high spiritual mastery.

(source: color-meanings.com)

The reason I so wanted to explain the rainbow's significance to you, is that it can also appear as a direct message from above that "all is well." I have maintained a Yogic lifestyle for close to 25 years, so knowing this gives me great comfort as I enter this last phase of Dad's life, by his side all the way.

Please trust in your own signals and messages, as they are ever present once we begin to trust and soften our gaze.

A sky full of rainbows to you.

Warrior

Today was a challenging morning! I walked into my dad's room and did not see him where he normally is waiting for me, either in his recliner chair or wheelchair. I looked in the bathroom and no Dad. I glanced at his bed and much to my shock he was lying still. I waited to see him breathe and quietly exited his room.

I was furious, to say the very least, as part of Dad's care involved his being assisted in getting ready at 8:00 a.m. at the latest. I felt very emotional at the sight of my father so helpless in his bed.

I took a few minutes to force myself to deep breathe so I wouldn't lose my cool with the director. I approached his open door and asked if I could enter, to which he said sure.

I mindfully and slowly said that Dad was neither up, dressed nor bathed. It was by now close to 9:00 a.m. and the breakfast room began clearing by 9;30-10:00 to prepare for the lunch crowd of seniors who dined early.

I asked him for his support in seeing that my father was assisted by 8:00 as he was an early riser to begin with. He started saying that maybe my dad wanted to sleep.

The warrior in me reared her head and I took several deep breaths before continuing. I reminded the director that my dad was living there for the assistance. I also said Dad needed to eat, following his medications, to remain healthy.

He shifted his blame from my dad to the caregivers. I once again felt the warrior and protector of my elderly father emerge, as well as for the hard working care givers!! I knew I had to keep my cool. but trust me. it was hard. He said he would look into it and send someone at once, which he did.

As I jogged down the three hallways, I felt both frustration and sadness for my dad in this very vulnerable state. Dad could no longer get out of his bed unassisted, dress himself or shower without help. He had been totally independent just seven months prior, and I could barely imagine how trapped he had to feel.

I appeared in the room and heard the caregiver helping him way too fast. My dad kept saying, "Ouch, you are hurting me," with simultaneous calls on the walkie talkies. Caregivers truly have the short end of the stick as they are underpaid and over worked.

The daughter, protector, human, advocate and warrior again surfaced. I literally self-talked myself out to the hallway to get a hold of my upset and disappointment in his care.

When I returned ten minutes later, Dad was ready, yet looked strained, likely from the rushing to get ready. I cheerfully said that we could go for a nice breakfast and he just nodded. It truly tugged at my heart. I pushed Dad to the dining room and speedily got his cereal and yogurt so he could get started. The irony is that I had just told one of the caregivers the day before that Dad liked being up early.

The main issue for me was that my dad was at the mercy of the staff. You may also have experienced this tango of wanting to get upset yet knowing calmness will be more effective. Many of you, like me may be somewhat new at this role. It is impossible to be in perfect balance or response with each new curve ball.

Please go gentle first with yourself and then with the powers that be. My Grandma Helena used to tell us as kids, "You attract more bees with honey." The meaning is sweetness begets sweetness Dear Ones.

The interesting thing about a warrior is that by definition it is a person who fights in battles and is known for having courage and skill (*Merriam-Webster dictionary)

A spiritual warrior is different. In Buddhism, they are the ones who combat the Universal enemy: self-ignorance. A spiritual warrior is a heroic being with a brave mind and ethical impulse.

I was somewhere between the two different types of warriors, which you may be too, depending on the circumstances that you are in .

The caregivers pulled me aside and said, "We are sorry, but we are understaffed." I expressed gratitude for their help and certainly no blame. The issue was that they were understaffed and not doing much to rectify it on the management levels. The caregivers were frustrated too.

My dad was now both comfortable and familiar with the staff and "his apartment," as he called it. To move him would be an impossibility as he was physically and cognitively declining before my eyes.

The priority was my dad's care and overall comfort. I had little to no interest in ANY conversations with the administrators of "he said, she said," otherwise known as blame or deflecting their responsibility.

Many of you reading this are also likely going through this delicate dance of warrior child, spouse, partner, or friend. The challenge is to quiet down the emotions and stay steady with the request for help or the need at hand. It sure isn't easy, friends!

I just want to extend my heart to those of you going through this. The best advice that I can offer is to "pause and collect yourself," before responding. I am grateful that I have the tools needed to pause and settle myself down. Still, I, like you, am a human and at times feel like losing my cool, many times a week!

Luckily, my dad knew little of what was happening as I tried my best to shield him from any external stress. He is weak, at times unclear and elderly. My heart tries its very best to comfort, alleviate, and soothe his weary soul.

May you be blessed with inner strength and the "pause between the breath."

Captivity

I look forward to the weekend when my husband, Peter, gives me a much needed break as caregiver, daughter and advocate for my dad. On this cool and crisp lazy Sunday, I received a call saying Dad was unwell. I literally froze, I suppose in fear and anxiety.

Dad's few freedoms were going to the dining room for meals and being pushed around town in his wheelchair. The nurse informed my husband that Dad had severe diarrhea and had been up four times at night. My poor father who can no longer walk the ten steps to his bathroom needs a caregiver to assist him. They are over worked and understaffed in the best circumstances, so this was yet again a major setback.

I contacted his physician who kindly said she would send a private RN (registered nurse) on Monday. Sadly, the residents could not have their meals in the dining room if they had diarrhea. I understood the reasoning on that. It could be both embarrassing as well as unpleasant for the other residents dining.

My dad who is not the greatest drinker of any kind is now at risk for dehydration. I had recently gotten Dad a variety of Gatorade to help him stay hydrated. The risk for seniors getting dehydrated is high. If a senior has diarrhea he is at further risk for dehydration as well as kidney issues.

My dad understood why he had to dine in his room and was agreeable. What truly broke my and Peter's heart is that he loves two things in particular: Going for meals in the cheerful "restaurant" as he calls it and going all through town in his wheelchair.

My dad is in captivity in his small room, and there is little that we can do to change or fix this for now. It simply is another sign that he is declining, as he eats the same foods daily. The presence of blood in his stool is also concerning. When a senior is on a blood thinner and his levels are not at a therapeutic level, bleeding can and does occur.

In the case of my almost 81-year-old daddy, he is sedentary most of the day due to his previous fall and fracture. The best possible outcome is that it is a 24-hour stomach bug, which I hope and pray to God that it is. I have a stirring and unsettling feeling that it is not that and I hope my intuition is wrong this time. My dad loves to eat and snack and now is captive to liquids to help alleviate his diarrhea.

I have packed up my trunk with some dominoes, cards and DVD's to fill his time. I also feel afraid as he is already so very frail. To take away his two pleasures of eating and outdoor field trips brings me to tears.

Whatever you are going through, similar to this or not, the best help I can offer you is to force yourself to stay in the moment. The moment allows us to be present and focused. The mind has a way to take us quickly to the past or future which mostly adds to the stress.

I invite you to try and have a cup of chamomile tea, light a pretty candle and watch a funny show. I am about to do the same to relax both my mind, body and spirit.

With love to you.

Caregivers

Most of us have had an experience with a caregiver or an idea of what that entails: I did too! In my humblest opinion, caregivers are the secret angels that allow for our loved ones to carry on. I well understand that there are a wide range of good, kind, loving, abrasive, and skilled caregivers! I have met the gamut and the range of these unsung heroes. The caregivers who have pierced the lining of my heart are the ones who love what they do genuinely. It is not an easy job by any stretch of the imagination to dress, shower, feed and, do most tasks for a senior or loved one in need. Caregivers are necessary and without the ones my dad has (in addition to me), he would not be here. Showing respect and allowing for dignity for someone who has lost most of theirs is an art form. One such lady, I will call "Jen," would shave my dad daily and then hand him the warm wash cloth to assist her in his grooming. This may sound trite, yet he felt that he was helping her and very much looked forward to her visits. Trust your parent's feedback when he tells you someone is rough or unkind. I was shocked in the early months to learn from Dad that someone had spoken horribly to him. Just because a senior or loved one is unwell, does not mean he deserves poor treatment. I cannot urge you enough to pay close attention to the feedback. I started making unannounced visits, which served two purposes. One, Dad felt safe and secure, and secondly, the few bad apples behaved better not knowing when I would appear!!! Caregivers often get paid poorly for doing a very needed job. Asking them about how they are doing as well as inquiring about their families helps show appreciation. I have found that keeping small candies in a jar is so much appreciated. I also make it a point to remember their names and details about their lives. The interaction with one's caregivers is somewhat fleeting. The relationship greatly impacts your loved one's daily existence profoundly at times. By the way, I am a caregiver too who did not realize it until six months into overseeing my dad's daily care!! One day, a staff member where Dad lived told me I was an excellent caregiver. It had never occurred to me that I, too, was indeed that. I had to adjust my role as doting daughter with that of Dad's caregiver to be effective. An example of this is when I help Dad with his shoes on. I am focused and in the caregiver role. When we are out in nature, I am simply his daughter spending time with him. Caregivers are perhaps the most underappreciated people I have come to know in the caring of my daddy. Please consider spending a few extra minutes saying thank you as well as engaging them in conversation that matters to them too. May you be blessed with loving, kind caregivers!

Divine Grace

Today was a day I was dreading. The day began with a heavy rain, and it was cold. A magnificent rainbow appeared and I took pictures of it to share with my dad. The previous day my dad was confined to his room as he had severe diarrhea. I was very worried that today he would be also being in a similar state. I walked reluctantly through the corridors with a feeling of dread and love.

I backtracked to the nurses' room, realizing I needed to know how my dad was first. The nurse told me Dad did not have diarrhea and I hugged her. She instructed me to give Dad oatmeal, toast and apple juice. I was absolutely beyond thrilled to hear this.

As I entered Dad's room he said, "Suzanne, I am so happy to see you again!" I had been off for two days, resting and looking after myself. I was well aware that when I was gone even for a few days, Dad missed me very much. My husband, Peter, lovingly took my shift to keep Dad engaged and in good company.

I told Dad that we were able to go to "the restaurant," as he affectionately called the dining room where all the meals were served.

I packed up the backpack, a blanket, a warm scarf, hat and Dad's sunglasses. I wheeled Dad to the dining room and put his breaks on. I went to get him a decaffeinated tea, plain cheerios (sans milk) and crackers. The servers knew my Dad's breakfast by heart, so I quietly went into the kitchen to tell them of the changes.

Dad usually shared my almonds with me as he waited for his breakfast, but today he could not. As Dad ate his oatmeal, bagel and jam, I was teary. The little things that we take for granted, like eating what one likes was in my thoughts. I was so grateful that Dad was not confined to his room. I felt elated. So simple and yet so freeing for him.

After breakfast, I bundled Dad up and pushed him with much more speed as the clouds were looming in the distance. I felt a sense of pure joy at the blessing of being able to take Dad in the morning crisp, fresh air.

As I pointed out to Dad the raging creek that days before was almost empty, he smiled. Divine grace had set in and Dad and I were in mostly silent for the few miles. I asked Dad if he wanted to get a fresh baguette and we aimed for the shopping center peacefully and in gracefulness.

Dad picked out several rolls, butter and a box of Ritz crackers. I parked Dad carefully under a covered table. He loved his large baguette and I joked with Dad that it wasn't as good as "Boudin" in Cupertino. I ran into a sandwich store and got Dad a Gatorade being aware he needed the electrolytes.

A young couple with their son sat near us. Dad watched the toddler closely. The parents said he was named Benjamin and was one year old. I asked if Dad could give him a pack of his crackers. The small child smiled at Dad which was as genuine as you can get, The Mom told Dad her son was just beginning to walk and brought the dear little boy next to Dad. She said "Benjamin give Mr. Jerry your beautiful smile," and he did. It got very cold so we packed up and left.

I asked Dad if he'd enjoyed himself, and he said, "very much," which again felt like "Divine Grace" to me.

I hope and pray that you, too, will have these tender and poignant moments amidst the storms. It takes breathing in gratitude and exhaling fear to truly embrace these rare and special blessed moments spent with the ones you love.

Champagne

Hey, I know what you are thinking!!! You were hoping this was about sipping champagne and indulging during these uncertain times?! Champagne Cafe is one of Dad's and my favorite bistros. Every summer and fall, Dad and I would go there together. Dad would always order the same thing: a large baguette with cream cheese or jelly. An herbal tea too. The real reason I suppose Dad liked going here so much was the beautiful array of pastries. They ranged in color from pastel pink to vibrant reds and greens. A real feast for the senses. On our last visit, they had beautiful leaf shaped sprinkle cookies. Dad always said "it's almost too pretty to eat it, Suzanne!" Dad then gobbled up every morsel of the shiny masterpiece. Today Dad pointed to the road leading near The Champagne Cafe. We had only gone there once since he moved here. I was sure Dad didn't recognize the proximity to the Cafe. We approached the Cafe, and tears filled my eyes. The only other time we'd passed by, Dad had wanted to "go home." This morning was different and Dad said yes to going in. In prior visits, I vividly remember his carefully pressed pale yellow long sleeved Oxford shirt, khakis and a belt. Today was markedly different as Dad was in a wheelchair, navy athletic shirt, sweats and tennis shoes. I brought Dad close to the glass pastry counter and pointed out the leaf cookies. Much to my surprise he said he wanted a yellow one. Dad and I sat at an outdoor table in the shade. I asked him if he remembered this place and he said yes. Happily, Dad ate his sprinkled leaf cookie and apple juice. A young couple next to us took our picture. I wanted to someday be able to see us together at his favorite Irvine cafe. Some people enjoy a good bottle of champagne to relax or celebrate with loved ones. For me, I will take Champagne Cafe with my dad by my side any day of the week. Cheers!

Anchor

When I think of my last 30 years, there is one person who has been by my side like no other. He is my husband Peter. He and I met when I was 17 and he was 19 in a study program in California. Peter was born and raised in the northeast of England, a world away from where I was born. When we met, we instantly had a strong and familiar connection. In Judaism the word is "B'Sheirit," or Fate. After our month long program, Peter returned to Newcastle Upon-Tyne England. We were both heartbroken. It was like for the first time in my young life, someone really understood me and I him: it was a mutual feeling. I won't spend your time on our three decades together. He is simply my anchor in life. Period. We have gone through the ups and down that most of you experience too. He is a gem and a rare one at that! When my dad fell in April, I was distraught and shaken up pretty badly. He offered reassurance that he would care for our then 16-year-old son as long as I needed to be by Dad's side. Peter also has a close relationship with my dad as well as our entire family. He cried when I told him what had occurred.

Peter and Dad would spend hours sitting in our family room discussing world affairs, which I avoided. They also enjoyed a good meal too. I cannot stress enough that caring for an ill or injured loved ones is so very difficult. Peter made the amount of time I was away from my youngest son and home bearable. I am a very devoted mother and was worried that Riley wouldn't eat, let alone have gas in his car. Yes, I admit: he's the youngest, and I hover far too much. Peter is my anchor and I pray that you too can find yours. I often felt that I was at sea without a rudder, and he would call or appear. My anchor's name is Peter, and he is my very best friend and husband too: THANK YOU ❤

Rise Up

In the early morning hours sometimes I wake up with a racing heart thinking about my dad. I place my right hand on my heart and my left one over it. I consciously breathe in calmness and exhale fear before getting out of my comfy bed. Trust me guys, this one to two minute exercise makes all the difference when you are dealing with stress of any kind. On other mornings, I feel like staying under my comforter and sleeping all day to avoid remembering my dad isn't well. It takes strength to "rise up," and meet each new day, especially when death is looming. Another way I raise my energy field and spirit is to say out loud, "Thank you, thank you, thank you!" I also pray out loud that my dad has no physical or mental suffering today, that he is at peace and comfortable. This takes practice and discipline to do, as it is easy to fall into anxiety and a depressed state over your loved one's ailing health. Another helpful tip is that when you go into the shower start it out cold. That helps to awaken your sensory system. Playing music also is helpful, as it can help you to connect with different feeling states. For me listening to Josh Groban helps to pull out my sorrow as well as joy. Whatever it takes to help support you during this time, use those tools.

May you rise up to meet this new day with love in your heart and strength in your conviction.

Service

One day on a particularly crisp morning, I heard a song in my head. I rubbed my head and even shook it, thinking I was just tired. Again distinctly, I heard the words clearly and this time listened. As I carefully pushed my dad forward, this familiar song reemerged. I recognized it, yet didn't know the words well enough to recall its origin. By early afternoon as I collapsed into our weathers cigar chair, I heard it once again. Guys, when all else fails, ask Siri (your iPhones best friend). I googled the lines and out pops: St. Francis of Assisi-13th Century. The words which were so soothing. I had heard them on Singh Kaur's C.D a year ago and many times prior. I had this strong sense that I was guided to hear it by my beloved spiritual teacher, Yogi Bhajan who was such a rich part of my life. Here is its entirety, as I hope & pray it offers you too comfort! Lord, make me an instrument of Thy peace; Where there is hatred, let me sow love; Where there is injury, pardon; Where there is doubt, faith; Where there is despair, hope; Where there is darkness, light; And where there is sadness, joy. O Divine master, Grant that I may not so much seek to be consoled as to console; To be understood, as to understand; To be loved, as to love; For it is in giving that we receive, It is in pardoning, that we are pardoned, And it is in dying that we are born to eternal life. Amen

Messages of Hope and Love

My favorite places to replenish were the garden centers. I didn't necessarily purchase items, just walked around. After a very taxing day of Dad's health remaining in a delicate state, I was fried. As I drove to Orchard Supply, an idea came to me. I purchased a small bag of blank white gardening stakes $1.49.

I went to my car and gathered all the sharpies I had and began writing messages:

LOVE
HOPE
SUPPORT
KINDNESS
RESPECT
SMILE
JOY
DREAM
BELIEVE
INSPIRE
CREATE
LAUGH
FAITH
FAMILY

I went home to eat my lunch and write a bit too. I couldn't wait to hide them on the edges of the entry to the senior home to brighten their day. Wherever inspiration, hope and love come to you, please share it with others in your life. Some people view seniors as "the invisible" part of society due to their age and appearance and often frailty too. I don't see it that way, and hopefully you don't either. People are people, and all of us regardless of our ages or health needs, want and require hope and love.

While my small idea didn't take much time or money, I know it cheered some people up. The next day, I saw a lovely couple I knew who resided there. They had found the love and respect stakes I placed outdoors where they frequently sit! It takes so little to bring messages of hope and love to others. I warmly invite you to spread that love as much as you possibly can because yes, it has value and can create hope and love for others.

Heroes

I have always appreciated firemen. Firemen are committed to the safety, health and well-being of our communities. They also exude confidence and strength which are appealing qualities to have.

As I was waiting in Panera Bread (a local restaurant), to pick up my son's favorite "mac & cheese," I noticed a group of fireman. I sheepishly approached their table and offered thanks for their help the previous day, when a senior at my Dad's community fell and needed to be checked out.

They said, "That is our job," to which I said, "Yes, and we are so grateful for your service."

I went back in line and purchased a bag of freshly baked chocolate chip cookies for the small group of five. They said, "Thank you for your kindness," which was ironic as I was acknowledging theirs. I smiled and could feel my cheeks fill to crimson shades.

There are many types of heroes that we come across daily. I invite you to consider taking time to thank those that you come across with a word or a gesture. It isn't necessary to buy anything, yet I thought the cookies looked so yummy that I couldn't resist purchasing them for these gallant men.

The young man who came to assist me when I was trying to comfort the senior who had fallen was a hero too. I would not have been able to lift him up without his physical strength.

The man who stood with my dad as I bolted across the busy street was also a hero. He made it possible for me to assist someone in need, as I would have never left my dad unattended in his wheelchair.

I give tremendous thanks to all the heroes who have shown up these last six months since my dad's fall. You become more aware of their presence when you are directly needing their assistance. I am grateful that the fire station is located across the street from Dad's senior home. The manner in which I have witnessed them interact with my dad as well as other seniors is touching. These large framed, strong men speak respectfully and kindly: THANK YOU very much!!

Wherever You Go, There You Are!!!

One thing that I have learned this last 1/2 year caring for my dad is this: I am a kind and thoughtful person. I have always deflected praise and compliments as I used to feel shy about "receiving" praise for what seemed second nature to me.

In the mornings as I got Dad his starting course for breakfast, I was constantly up and down, assisting others in need. It's just who I am. One particular day, I saw a woman searching for a place to sit. After 9:30 most residents had eaten and many tables were still being cleaned up. The service for lunch began soon thereafter, so seniors arriving later had to look to share a seat at an occupied table. I bolted up and gently brought her to our table. I brought her the last cinnamon muffin and asked the server to please take her order.

The lady told my dad, "You sure have a thoughtful daughter," which made my dad smile brightly. We sat a few more minutes and I collected Dad's belongings for our walk around the neighborhood.

Despite its being November, we were experiencing a small "heat wave," and the morning sun could be depleting for most. As we passed a gardener who was planting red and white begonias, I stopped. I carefully retrieved the small water bottle with a small chocolate. I smiled and continued down the block.

Please consider packing an extra drink or snack when out and about town. It is often the case that you will bump into another person who would benefit and appreciate your kind and thoughtful gesture.

Halloween had just passed and all the candies were 75% off currently. I purchased a few bags of the green M&M's as I knew the front desk staff liked them.

Small acts of daily kindness are so very important. They help us all feel more connected and present to each other, as well as appreciated.

When I was leaving Dad's senior residence, a woman gave me a bottle of water. As I turned the hall I saw a woman pushing a large cart with a new resident's items. I extended the water bottle and she gratefully accepted it. If we all do our small part in sharing these simple gestures of kindness, we will be a more cohesive community, for sure.

Diplomacy

The three most diplomatic people in my life would be my husband, Peter, my Uncle Mike, and my eldest son, Zachary. My Uncle Mike has taught me over the years to "go to the balcony," before responding. Many scenarios have ensued these last six months that required me to be diplomatic. I for the most part I tried my very best to pause and look down at the situation from "the balcony." You may find, as I did, that in certain crisis states, sometimes we fall short of responding as well as we might like. We all have our different triggers or things that set us off. We also have different coping mechanisms to deal with stress. I would say I tried to be diplomatic and follow the model I have seen in action from my husband. It is very difficult to remain neutral when you are attempting to make quick decisions in life and death circumstances. My son, Zachary, in dealing with his siblings and even us, his middle aged parents, has his own natural finesse. I do not have a natural, diplomatic style although others who know me would disagree. I have tried to strengthen this muscle by "going to the balcony," the way my uncle taught me. You simply take a few minutes and try and look down at what's unfolding. I find that what helps me to be more diplomatic is to ask for a few minutes before responding or returning to the scene in question. This is not always possible as in the case when my dad fell. I do want to offer you hope and encouragement as the more you practice, the easier and more natural it becomes. Sometimes when I look back to the many meetings and one-on-ones with staff, I cringe at my responses. Please take it from me: this is new territory so be kind to yourself too!

Thanksgiving

It is not often that I celebrate both my birthday and Thanksgiving on the same day; this year was doubly special. My husband and daughter set up our dining room table with so much love, thought and color. There was a kiss birthday tiara and a "birthday girl badge." Balloons and banners filled the walls and ceiling too.

This had been the hardest seven months of my entire life. Everything in my entire life had changed as a result of my dad's fall and brain injury. I didn't sleep the same and I was constantly on ALERT. You may be experiencing this too, and my heart goes out to you with a big gentle embrace; it's tough for sure! Normally, my husband and kids know that I am not much of a gift person. In fact, I much prefer homemade cards. Seeing the flowers adorning our table and the gifts piled high, I was deeply touched.

This year was very different. Because of my dad's fall, I was constantly jotting down ideas and thoughts for how I could best help him, now so frail and at times so confused. There were days that I simply didn't know if my heart could handle another beat, yet it was strong and gratefully it could. I was thankful for each day in a way I had never known before. Tragedies have a way of dragging you through the fire and making you stand to attention. We drove to my dad's senior home to share a catered Thanksgiving meal. As much as I had hoped that Dad could go to my brother's, he simply was too unstable to travel the distance, let alone navigate a steep driveway and many stairs. I was aware of how anxious I felt walking through Dad's building. There was a very different feeling in the air today. Many, many people came to spend Thanksgiving day with their loved ones. Normally, during the week there were few visitors outside of myself, which always made me sad. The brightly colored fall decorations warmed up the dining room. When we entered Dad's room, he was all dressed up! The caregivers had clearly spent extra time placing Dad in a dress shirt and slacks. Dad seems so small in his chair with a large shirt almost swallowing him up, he was so thin now. My dad handed me a card and a pretty yellow orchid plant. My husband, Peter, had secretly gone the day before for Dad to sign a card. These days writing was an arduous task, so when I saw my dad's neatly written signature with my name, I nearly lost it. Dad had told Peter that "Suzie is like a fine wine. She just gets better with age." For a man who spoke few sentences these days, this was yet another blessing to hold on to and cherish. My son put his slender arm around me, as he understood my pain. Riley at 17 was more sensitive, strong and aware than most people I had met on my 52-year journey. I needed his strength. As we rounded the corner there were people all dressed up eagerly waiting to enter the dining room for their Thanksgiving day feast. I just burst into tears. I sucked in a huge amount of air and gathered all of my strength to regain my lost composure for my dad. He looked lost in this large crowd so I knelt down and held his cold and slender hand. The dining room was beautiful. Bright decorations and flowers created an warm and inviting ambiance. The napkins which were normally white were burgundy and gold. My dad sat at the head of our private table. He looked happy, yet overwhelmed. My husband explained the menu options and ordered for him. Dad loved the homemade corn muffins and I happily watched him devour three! As we sat at the table, I was mixed with both deep love, joy, and gratitude and sadness, too. My dad loved his colorful plate of food. Dad had been a vegetarian some 50 years, yet as a result of his brain trauma he sometimes asked for meat.

I requested from my family that we each go around the table saying something we were thankful for. Some answers were silly answers, but Dad and I offered thanks for each other. After a beautiful meal we all went outside to fresh air near the soothing water fountain. Dad instantly fell asleep after such a large meal. I was so, so thankful to be sitting together with Dad, Peter and two of our three kids. We brought Dad back to the room and I carefully got him more cozy clothes to wear. As I said goodbye, our eyes locked without a word: gratitude and love was being expressed and I was deeply thankful.

Exhale

I have been noticing for several weeks now that I am not fully exhaling. I feel at times I simply cannot breathe, and at other times that my breath is deep and rich with oxygen. The strange thing is that I am able to inhale and exhale very, very deeply due to my decades of practice. I am aware of my "holding my breath," when my dad shows any signs of distress. It makes sense to me now as I have not fully let go of my wish for Dad to be here and heal. My lack of a deep exhale or "holding my breath," partially in is related to not fully surrendering to my dad's failing health. There are days that I feel peace and acceptance, perhaps like many of you. Then it can flip flop to wanting my dad back, as he was, healthy, clear minded and walking. Please be extra gentle and kind to yourself when you come to the realization that you are not in full acceptance. It is a process that isn't arrived at overnight. With a deep exhale and a hug to you.

Actions Speak Louder than Words!

One thing you may have already found out in your journey is that actions speak louder than words. Nearly eight months since my dad's fall from grace, many people have fled the scene. While on a spiritual level I well understand that it brings up the big "D" word for many, so it's often easier to avoid. The "D" word of course is death and the mere echo of it can send people into hiding. I have had many close friends say I am here for you and care, yet rarely ask how I am managing this very challenging obstacle course. I also have noticed people will ask how my Dad is and when I answer honestly quickly deflect the point that my Dad is very quickly declining in all ways. Perhaps you are also encountering this disappointment? All I can share is that what helps me is the understanding that people can only act from where they are in their own evolvement emotionally and perhaps spiritually too. Some days I get upset or hurt that those closest to me seem oblivious to how much my life has changed in the course of eight months, since Dad's fall and brain injury. Actions speak louder than words for me. A phone call, a note, or even offering to visit my dad is an action. For the most part of this journey, aside from a core group of friends and family members, I walk this hard and rocky path alone. My wish for you is that you are surrounded by supportive people who act in a manner that helps you. All blessings and love to you.

Say What You Need to Say

There is a very fine balance between telling Dad what I am grateful for and not wanting him to think his end is near. The way I have been sharing my feelings of love, gratitude and appreciation with Dad is slowly. Yesterday, I shared with Dad my fond memories of hiking with him at the Sierra Club. I told Dad that my love of nature came from him. I also spoke to Dad about how I had become an excellent researcher of sorts, as he had ingrained in my head to always question a diagnosis with more data. I also wanted to make certain that Dad knew how blessed I was to be spending all these hours and days so close by his side. Holding back feelings of love, gratitude, and appreciation doesn't serve a purpose. Yes, it can be very emotional; yet it will help you feel complete after. We never know what day or time our loved ones will pass. That has been a great fear of mine in recent years. That is why I am sharing with you this important part of the journey. I also told Dad I loved him with all my heart and soul. He said, "Ditto and thank you." These days' conversations don't occur for my dad. I felt the immediacy of sharing what was in my heart as painful as it was. Please know that our hearts carry so much depth and capacity to endure our emotions. I wish for you that you say whatever is in your beautiful hearts.

Elder Abuse is Shocking!

It has taken me two weeks to write about this awful experience. I have had moments ranging from disbelief to real anger.

I had returned my dad to his room after a beautiful morning spent in nature together. Dad was tired so I pressed his bracelet pendant which signals for the caregiver to arrive to his room. They have 12-14 minutes to show up, and it is always apparent how understaffed they are.

I took my backpack, which I always hang on Dad's coat rack, to pick up his mail and put it carefully away. I also took his trash cans as I do not like to leave them full.

When I returned minutes later, the caregiver was yelling, at my dad saying, "Honey, help me, my arm is hurt; help me."

I still don't know how I had the composure not to totally lose it upon hearing her YELL at my dad. I said my dad needed *her* help, which is why he lived there.

She continued yelling, now at me, "Your dad shouldn't be living here. He needs to be living somewhere else!"

I looked her straight in the eye and said I was sorry her arm was hurt but that she was not to yell at my bad again.

"I'm sorry that I am not perfect like you," she said.

I quickly told her that I was neither perfect nor willing to allow another minute of her raised voice or inappropriate dialogue. She did not back down.

I told her that I did not appreciate her calling my father "honey" in a loud and aggressive tone.

She said she did not know his name!

I said he had lived there for five months and to address him as Jerry or Dr.

Again, this woman called him "honey."

I got Dad settled and he asked "what happened?" I told him not to worry that I would handle it.

I was absolutely certain that, had I been quick enough to tape this, anyone viewing it would say this indeed was "elder abuse." I went into the director's office and asked to speak with him about what just happened. I have a very good memory and repeated the exact details. He said that he would take care of it through human resources. I made it clear that I would not let this go. She was not to enter my dad's room again. He promised he would comply.

What was most shocking was that he tried to suggest that this caregiver was "one of his best," and having a bad day! While I don't enjoy conflict, my gut told me I had to be diligent in following through with a written report.

My dad no longer had the ability to stand up for himself either physically or mentally. I most certainly was not going to allow this treatment of my beloved father.

I went to my car and literally shook thinking about this truly abusive encounter!

I called the director back at 4 to make certain he made his phone call to human resources. He told me that the caregiver admitted exactly what I had said.

If you are going through the care of your loved one, please be certain to write or record any incidents that are in this category of elder abuse.

The next morning, before I saw my dad, the director told me it was being investigated. I asked him how he would feel having a caregiver yelling at his parent and he said "not good."

Two weeks later, and the caregiver is still working there! While I have a patient and forgiving heart, this was something I could not allow for my dad.

Please know that there are many resources, like an ombudsman, which is a licensed volunteer who can help you investigate anonymously. Unfortunately, in my dad's case, we couldn't use this service as Dad would have had to recant what happened, which sadly he wasn't capable of.

I hope and pray for you that you don't encounter such a terrible situation. It brings up close and personal the need for a senior advocate, who has a strong voice to follow through when a parent can no longer speak up for his own human basic rights!

Grief

Most people think of grief as something you experience or face with the death of a loved one. I learned along this journey, that there are many stages of grief, even in life.

Elisabeth Kubler-Ross is a well-known author for writing about the 5 stages of grief:

1. Denial
2. Anger
3. Bargaining
4. Depression
5. Acceptance

In the beginning when Dad fell, I was unable to do anything but run on adrenaline and cry a lot. My brother asked me one day in the hospital cafeteria, "How is it possible, Sue, to cry that much and still have tears left?" He was saying it, I am certain, to add some humor. By then my eyelids were swollen and I had the appearance of someone who had been through a great deal. Truth is, I could barely look at my face in the mirror as it would make me cry even more seeing my duress!

I was unaware until a dear friend pointed it out that I was experiencing deep grief. Having experienced the death of loved ones, I was familiar with Dr. Kubler-Ross' five stages. I simply was unaware that I was experiencing grief. Facing the sudden shock of your loved ones being seriously injured or incapacitated, you will undoubtedly feel the heavy weight of that emotional impact. Grief for me, began to unfold when the dad I knew so well became a very different person. The connection and closeness we shared remained very much the same. He knew I was his devoted daughter, and I knew I was his anchor.

My dad was always a very strong minded individual, in part due to his intellectual genius. He could pretty much talk about any subject ranging from global warming, nature, physics, and math to Krishnamurti. He'd explained to me during our three-day visit in February that he appreciated my wanting to clean his apartment and shop for him, but that it made him feel as if he wasn't doing things right. This conversation would haunt me, as it highlighted Dad's darkest fears, which we were now facing head on: that of losing his priceless independence.

Speaking to him daily about life, his grandchildren, his current mathematic endeavors to crack a code, had been a part of my daily life. Now, our interactions were steeped in helping him survive this nightmare. Helping Dad to have the best possible chance for a quality life, which he deserved, was now the central part of both of our lives. Grieving for the father who would have inevitably told me exactly what to do, had this been someone else was hard for me to accept or digest.

I am sure many of you reading this can relate to wanting "your old life back," which includes how you related to your family member. What I can share with you is however you are feeling is completely fine. When you are ready to accept your "new norm," then you will. It took me almost six months to even begin to embrace that life as I knew it was no longer the same.

When one is experiencing grief, what truly helps is having a strong support system around you. I quickly learned who had the capacity to BE there for me, when I had not much to offer in return. Sometimes, you may find that there are some surprising treasures that await you in who shows up for you when you are down. I feel enormously blessed and grateful to the family, friends and community that rally around me still and therefore my daddy.

Silence is Golden

My dad and I have shared daily phone calls for the last many years. We talked about the family, his book club, friends and daily happenings. This all changed in an instant on April 12, 2016! I must admit that at first, I was very loquacious around Dad. I was trying to help stimulate his brain into action. I tried music, books, videos and long talks with interesting topics. After two months, I realized that Dad's processing ability had greatly diminished. He could handle exactly one slow conversation at a time. He also could only manage one simple command spoken quite slowly with a five to ten second pause to answer. This was harrowing to witness, let alone accept. My dad had entered UCLA at 16 and was an academic prodigy of sorts. Explaining things at this new pace was very hard to adjust to. Dad would grow frustrated when I would forget and start talking too fast. It had to be hell for him to adjust, as he had prided himself on his intellectual giftedness for most of his life. When Dad moved to be closer to the family it seemed like a great new beginning. That hopefulness in what Dad would be able to do and his overall healing faded to black with his second big fall. The interesting thing is that when you are adjusting to a new mental and physical range, there are still gifts in that new space. In month two, Dad seemed to be talking less and I had no idea why. Again I tried to find answers for his limited speaking and there were no medical answers to follow! It struck me one breakfast that I didn't need to fill the space with words anymore. Once this clicked in my psyche, Dad and I developed our own "secret sign language." Dad could simply look at me and I knew what he was needing or thinking! I also added hand signals like hearts or I love you sign language, which he loved. It most certainly was an adjustment as part of me missed my dad's words and many helpful talks. Now Dad needed me to be there fully present in silence. The miraculous thing is, on some days, out of nowhere, my dad's language would return for a minute and he would ask some relevant question. I quickly had to let go of his fluency lasting, as it was like a short circuit that occasionally found its breaker. I have great empathy for all of you going through this part of the journey. Please know that it is perfectly human to long for the person who used to be. The phrase, "silence is golden," actually means something to me now.

I can tell by my dad's facial mannerisms almost precisely what he is saying. I am enjoying this sacred ground we walk in silence together shrouded in great love too.

My Angel Daughter

To be honest with you, this was one of the chapters I put off writing the longest. Dad and I had developed a routine together and were very much "a team." We didn't need a ton of words to communicate and enjoy our hours of daily visits.

My dad was never into "spiritual lingo," although I certainly was and he knew it.

I was a person who had always used positive language. I also believed in other realms as well as angelic presence in my life and others'. I had just returned from my first week away from Dad since he moved to Southern California. It was painstaking for me to get on the plane and travel some 3,000 miles to my dear friend's home. My friend had lost her sister, mother and uncle all in the course of a year's time. I had promised to spend time with her as her sister (who had tragically passed) was my dearest friend in my early "yogic years."

I remember sitting at the gate and feeling pangs of fear, excitement and worry. I prayed that my dad would not feel abandoned as I had been the one constant in his daily life now for many months.

After an incredible five days, I returned relaxed and restored. When I entered Dad's room, he shook his head and said emotionally, "My angel daughter is here!" To say I almost lost it would be mild. I knelt down and hugged my dad. He did not let go of me for minutes, which made me cry. I told Dad that I was always with him even when we were apart. I explained that the close bond and love that he and I shared was always with me. He nodded.

A year ago when my dad checked out a book from the library on Buddhism, I was thrilled. A week later Dad shared that he like most of Buddhism's teachings but was really deterred by the "reincarnation" notion. I told Dad to take the stuff he liked and could relate to and discard the rest.

He was a scientist to his core. I was his spiritual daughter who worked hard at being in service to others. I also did my best to heal whatever wounds I carried, so I could be more present and at peace.

Dad at breakfast told me that I was the one person he looked forward to seeing more than anyone because "I was his angel in every way," I

145

thanked Dad and reminded him that I had some bad days too, and he smiled. I also reminded Dad not to say I was his favorite when other family members were present in order not to hurt their feelings.

Please cherish the moments and memories that are organic in nature as well as heartwarming. I will always remember my dad's face when he told me that was his "angel daughter," for all the days of my blessed life.

The Descent

I have been feeling a bit whimpery these last few days around my dad. I do my very best not to cry around him, as he has enough happening. This morning when I went into my shower, I just burst into tears. I kind of scared myself because it was 6 a.m. and nothing really provoked my tears. First, I resisted the wave of emotion demanding me to release it. (Trust me friends, it takes so much more energy to resist our feelings versus breathing into them.) After a very exhausting cry, I fed our six-month-old kitten, Pepper. There is something very therapeutic about a young cat that follows you around. My friend, Danny, and I speak most mornings as he drives to work. I shared my "shower cry," with him, and he listened. His next insight hit me so hard that I felt dizzy! "Your dad is dying. Of course your years are coming up." I cried ten more minutes in the car and actually felt better. Wherever you are at on your descent, please be gentle with yourself, as this is very hard to go through. At breakfast my dad was quieter and seemed more "out of it." I couldn't help but hear Danny's true, yet haunting, words. I was grateful he spoke them as, believe it or not, I don't think I had FULLY gotten that Dad was, indeed, dying. I know from the Metaphysical perspective we are all dying a bit daily, yet Dad's decline was fast upon me. We spent an extra hour at the lake, one of Dad's favorite places to be. As he napped, I looked at him and studied his face. Dad looked tired and worn out. I fed him some chocolate mints, water and his favorite, peaches. Walking Dad back to his senior home, I felt as though I was watching us from above—there we were, Dad and I, moving down the street as a single unit, a team. When we returned, Dad said he was tired. I never left him without a kiss on his cheek or an "I love you." These past few days had shown me Dad was descending quickly and I was scared and yet fully present with him. Please know that as you enter the last stage of your loved ones' life, to practice care and support for yourself. Having friends and family around makes a big difference, guys. I am going to get a 30 minute foot rub that my Uncle Mike recommended today. Going downhill requires even more care and oxygen. Being mindful of breathing deeply, breaks and proper hydration & nutrition is imperative. Watching my dad descend so rapidly makes me feel some days like running away and hiding in a cave. The truth is I

147

cannot avoid this very painful chapter of my dad's impending death. With love and support, Suzie

Letting go

A very hard part of these last eight months has been letting go of being there daily. I hit a point of pure exhaustion a week ago after dealing with the "elder abuse" trauma and subsequent drama from its fallout.

I was fortunate to have enough self-awareness to recognize the signs of my "caregiver burnout." I made an appointment with a woman who has spent 30 years as a caregiver and assisting others in their last stage of life through in home hospice care. At first I was reluctant to even meet with her, as I was almost feeling guilty for feeling "burnt out." After sharing with her my experience she looked at me and said, "What are you willing to let go of?"

I knew immediately that I needed to hire a kind and professional person to supplement my dad's care so I could have a few days off. I set up an interview to meet with two private agency caregivers. I felt a mix of anxiety as well as hopeful relief.

She also asked me if I could look outside of myself and see what I had done these last eight months. I quickly welled up with tears SEEING the love, devotion, strength and immense time that I had spent for and with my dad. I was tired just reviewing it from a spectator's vantage point.

I went to my car after the consultation and wrote down what I was willing to let go of:

1. Going to see Dad daily.
2. Managing all of his doctor, nurses, medications, supplies, caregivers and physical therapy.
3. Doing every single aspect of his care (minus the finances that my sister-in-law graciously handled!)

The following many days, I kept true to my promise for my own self-care and well-being. I interviewed the two caregivers and hired one on a trial basis. I also used my many decades of breathing techniques to quell my fears that Dad would object.

Today was the first "normal day," that I have had in almost a year.

I drove to Laguna Beach and watched the waves crash along the shore. I attended my favorite chanting and Kirtan class and enjoyed it immensely.

When I returned hours later, I was thrilled to receive a text from the new caregiver saying that it went well.

I had to remind myself that I was of no use or support to my dad if I didn't restore my energy and take time off.

I can't tell you this is easy, the "letting go" of your loved ones every need, but trust me; it is necessary. This has been one of the hardest aspects of this process—letting go—and a huge life and spiritual lesson for sure.

I am looking forward to the next part of this journey, while having a much healthier balance for me too! I am very grateful that I was able to get help before I was flat lined.

Please make sure that you allow for time off and that you pay attention to the many apparent signs of "burn out."

With love and prayers to you.

I'm Walking Dad Home

One day a month ago, I thought I was losing my marbles. While I was pushing Dad in his wheelchair in the rain, I literally heard in my head "Suzie, you are walking Dad home." At first, I thought it was fatigue setting in as my hair was soaked and my hands slippery on the chair's handles. When Dad and I returned to his senior home I sat him before the fireplace. He did not get wet at all, as I had him bundled in a hat and blanket while he held the umbrella. As we sat quietly together and I sipped water again I heard, "You are walking Dad home." By the time I got Dad settled back in his room he was quite tired. As I walked slowly down the two corridors, I heard the same message fill my head. " You are walking Dad home." Sitting in my car with the heater blasting I understood the message from above. Dad was in no immediate health crisis, that wasn't the point. The meaning for me was that I was helping Dad literally walk home or to the next stage on his journey. I sat quietly for fifteen minutes before I felt grounded enough to drive. Truth be told, I was at first freaked out a bit by the intrusion of the message, yet grateful too. I have always been a believer in other, unseen realms. I have often accessed other places in my meditative practice as well as in nature. This time, though, the message was very real and deeply personal. My Dad was allowing me, and very much needing me, to "walk him home." Although the thought of him passing still scared me, I had slowly come to the space of taking things day to day to alleviate my concerns and fears. It's actually quite a profound and beautiful message to "walk our loved ones home." For me, it represents being fully present in the process as Dad faces his last chapter. My hope for you reading this is that you are able to trust the messages that may come in different forms. Blessings to you.

Epilogue

April 13th, 2017,

Thursday, was a typical day for Dad and me. I met him with an enthusiastic greeting in his senior home. We had a sweet breakfast together where I made even the minute seem like a special celebration. Fruit placed on a plate in a shape of the sun. At this point Dad just grinned at me and said, " How pretty, Suzanne," as I placed his white cloth napkin in his lap like the concierge of a chic restaurant. It was a warm spring morning and after pushing Dad along the creek, he said he was tired and wanted to go back to "his apartment." I had carefully made Dad believe he was in just that, a new apartment, as his greatest fear prior to his fall was that he be in some "assisted living senior home." He actually was living in an assisted senior home but my sister-in-law had found a place that was "resort style living," so it appeared more like a hotel/luxury apartment. My belief all along was that if Dad felt as "normal" as possible, then he would adjust and heal better. I asked Dad if he wanted an ice cream as it was warm and he nodded and grinned. We went through the frozen aisle of Ralph's Market and I carefully placed four of Dad's favorite ice creams in his lap. He intently looked over each wrapped treat and chose a Hagan Daz vanilla caramel bar with chocolate on the outside. Whenever we checked out, I always gave Dad the money and the item so he would feel more a part of things which he seemed to like. As we sat under the yellow umbrellas in the early day sun, tears filled my eyes. Dad looked at me concerned and I said I had once again gotten sunscreen in my eyes. I didn't want my dad to worry, and yet tears streamed down my face watching my frail daddy eat his ice cream bar with so much childlike joy. We returned to "his apartment," and a caregiver helped Dad to his "lift chair recliner." Dad almost always said, "Are you leaving me now?" despite the hours of our time together. Truth be told, this always felt like a fiery arrow through my heart as he was so close and attached to me and vulnerable too. I said, "Would you like me to read to you for a bit?" and he nodded sheepishly. My dad had been a great intellectual, and even after his brain injury liked hearing about new research. I read him his Harvard medical newsletter for senior men's health. He received so many top scholarly newsletters, and being healthy and informed were so important to Dad. As I sat knelt at his chair's side, he dozed off peacefully. I covered him in his light red blanket and kissed his check and quietly left his room.

Friday, April 14th

I left the house at 6:30 a.m. to sadly drive into Los Angeles to attend the funeral of a childhood friend, Larry who had died from a stroke, he was 52. It was an emotional day attending Larry's funeral and seeing his aged parents mourn their son's death along with childhood friends I had not seen in decades, since we all had gone our separate ways for college and life. I had packed a bag in case I would stay with Lisa and Steve, my dear friends. As people were getting ready to go to the gathering at Larry's parents' house, I got a very strong sense I needed to go straight home. I was in L.A's gridlock freeway traffic, yet felt this urgency to go home, not knowing what would unfold. When I arrived home, I was so emotionally drained, I showered and climbed into my bed.

Saturday, April 15th

I got up at my usual 5:45 a.m. and showered, meditated and left the house to go to CVS. Saturdays had recently become my "day off," as my husband Peter would take Dad to breakfast and his daily wheel chair stroll. I was getting my eight-year-old niece Easter goodies, when my cell rang. I immediately felt shaky and took the call outside. My dad's senior home was calling to say Dad woke up "choking and coughing," and he was in the ambulance en route to Hoag Hospital. I sat in my car and did my best to breathe deeply but felt a sense of raw terror engulf me. Peter was on his way, and I drove the 15 minutes to the emergency room. As I entered the room, I hugged my dad who looked terrible, compared to two days prior. I quickly went into comfort-and-calm-Dad mode. He struggled to answer as well as breathe! I told Dad he would be okay and just needed some rest and possibly medication but little did I really know what was about to unfold... The nurse asked to talk to me and explained what was happening to my beloved daddy. He had aspirated from his vomit and had both pneumonia and the flu. I literally crumbled to the floor and sat holding my knees on the ground. I asked how could Dad have pneumonia or the flu when he was immunized recently? She then explained in very scary terms he would likely not make it. As my mind tried to grasp this information, a doctor walked in my dad's make shift room. As he spoke, I could not believe that this was my dear friend John! I had totally forgotten he was a doctor at Hoag. I was still reeling from the morning's events. His face told me what my heart wasn't ready to face. By then, my twin brother had arrived, and he explained Dad's grim prognosis. Dad had a medical directive stating no heroic measures or breathing tubes, so his wishes were spelled out clearly. John said he would have a few days to live and he would make sure he was as comfortable as possible. He was moved to the fifth care which was like "hospice." The nurses were so kind and gentle it was really incredible in a tough situation. Dad was at first somewhat lucid and spoke to Peter with a few words. That part really messed with my mind, as he seemed well. Yet he was dying?!! I brought Dad's favorite red Stanford blanket so he wouldn't get confused. He had had that red soft blanket for the year since his fall and it seemed to be familiar to him as well as comforting. I called his younger kids (ages 27 and 29) to inform them of Dad's situation. They both flew in, and we got them a hotel literally across from the hospital parking lot. John was not only a dear friend but a very smart and warm physician. He spoke to me as a doctor and as a friend who knew me very well. He explained to me as I sobbed, that Dad would need to hear from me (his closest child) that it was okay to let go. Despite my dad's being on morphine, I could still very much see he was alive and that the light was on. John said it usually was two days with someone in dad's grave condition, and I said it would be longer. We all took time being with Dad. I would nap on a hospital bench in the garden as going home seemed too far away. I wanted to give Dad's other children time with him too. The nurse showed me how to move the guard rail down and I would touch Dad's face and play him "The Four Seasons" by Vivaldi. If I stopped touching his face or moved the music he would move and ever so slightly raise his eyebrow. I constantly told Dad to just rest as I comforted him with both by touching his face and talking. I wasn't sure I could tell him it was okay to let go, as selfishly, I didn't want to let go of my daddy!

Sunday, April 16th

The doctor and nurses told us to get them if we saw that Dad was in distress (breathing) or appeared in pain. My brother, Jamie, and I were the ones who were to determine if he needed more morphine, which was brutal for me as that would eventually kill him. I knew I had to have "the talk" with Dad about letting go but felt both nauseous and dizzy. With John, at the door, which I'd requested for strength, I sat near Dad and said the hardest words I had ever said. "Daddy, it's okay not to struggle so hard anymore. I will be okay and by your side. He lifted his left eyebrow and I continued, telling him he should just rest and listen to his music. I bit my check so hard to keep from bawling that I could taste blood in my mouth. I held Dad's hand and put on Beethoven's "Fur Elise," which is how Dad chose my middle name, "Elise." John (a saint) nodded at me and left the room. I stayed with Dad till he looked in a deep relaxed state and allowed for Daniel, his youngest son, to sit there too. As I took the five flights of stairs down to the garden, I felt so, so sad. How could Dad be on morphine and dying when he had just been eating ice cream three days before?! I lay down on the garden bench and literally fell asleep due to the toll of the emotions.

Monday, April 17th

Dad's eyes were still open, which was very confusing for me. I saw life, and therefore hope. Yet the doctors and nurses said he was dying. Dad had exceeded their expectations by still being very much alive day two. His heart rate was still that of a younger man, despite having his lungs being filled with fluid. Dad had always prided himself in healthy eating and daily exercise. To say that he was regimented in his care would be a gross understatement. On this day, I decided to wash his face and brush his hair. Others looked at me as if I was nuts. I always believed that if you looked better, you would feel better, so perhaps this would help Dad feel better? I found some beautiful reading videos with sound both of the sea and forest and played them for Dad who seemed to breathe better. I continued to speak reassuringly to Dad, telling him that his only job was to rest and listen to music. He did.

Tuesday, April 18th

Rachmaninov was Dad's favorite piano concerto, and I played it for him in the morning. By mid-day he seemed both in pain and to be breathing terribly. It was so excruciating to see my dad gasp for air. I just wanted to give him oxygen! The doctors were shocked Dad was day three and still showing a strong heart rate. They were talking about moving him to Hospice care. I said, "Not happening." I was able to lie next to Dad, leaning on the chair and the railing, and he seemed comforted. I just told Dad how much I loved him and played classical and peaceful tunes.

Wednesday, April 19th, 2017

I sprinted to the hospital an hour earlier as I felt Dad was weakening. This morning Dad looked more ashen and half there. I put a cool cloth that I had brought from home on Dad's forehead. He was burning hot. Everyone but me was to wear hospital masks when entering the room. I just couldn't wear it and talk normally to Dad and lay near him. I simply asked God to bless me without getting the flu or pneumonia, although was not immunized from. My intuition told me I would be fine and that being present for Dad without the mask was more important. I went to the cafeteria on my break and ate saltine crackers and Perrier water. I simply couldn't eat more. I was emotionally fraught and nauseous. As I lay outside on the bench, I heard a voice say, "It's time." ` I bolted and ran to the elevator and the entire way to Dad's fourth floor room. Surprisingly, no one was there. I shut the door. I looked at Dad and knew the voice I heard outside was timely. I climbed as close to Dad as I could and played Rachmaninov and touched his face gently. I literally could SEE Dad as a young boy running in a tall field of grass and wild flowers. I stayed focused on this SIGHT and told Dad his beloved Mommy Ruthie was at the end of the forked road waiting for him. I SAW her but not as I knew her—elderly and confused—but young and exuberant. I said, "Daddy, run to your mom and I will meet you there someday when it is also my time. As my dad's breathing seemed to strengthen I took every fiber of strength of my being and said, "Daddy, it's time to let go and be unencumbered. I will be okay."

A giant blue butterfly appeared and I told my dad, "It's true what the poets say Daddy; it's true." I then felt a strong wind. I said "Daddy, even a brilliant mind like yours wouldn't argue with the wind. It's okay, Daddy, let go now and you will come meet me there when it is my time." I then saw and heard my dad take his last breath. I cooled his clammy face down, brushed his hair, covered him with his red Stanford blanket and got the nurse. I then called my brother. When the young nurse (early 20"S) appeared, she said Dad was gone. I went for the first time into his bathroom and threw up and washed my face. I didn't recognize the face staring back at me... My brother appeared and he said a Jewish prayer and spoke to Dad. The nurse said she would have to do some things that I may not want to see. I hugged and kissed Dad for the last time, and my brother said he would handle the rest. I ran all the way to my car and opened all my windows and sobbed. My Daddy had died, but he had survived a year past a near fatal fall and head injury. For that I was so, so grateful.

My father did not want a funeral, just cremation. I ordered a bench though the city of Woodbridge that would be placed exactly where he and I would go weekly. The lake was a place where my dad seemed most at peace. The bench would take six to eight weeks to order and be installed at the precise spot Daddy so loved. July 15, 2017 Dad's bench memorial was placed. The plaque read; 12-7-35 to 4-19-17 Dr Gerald G. Comisar "Love is the Bridge." We love you, Daddy Dad's closest friends at The Atria, Gene and Loie, along with a small group of family, friends and caregivers (doctors, nurses and such). All sat nearby as people shared their stories of the good man who was my daddy. We took everyone to Dad's favorite Irvine restaurant, CPK (California Pizza Kitchen) for Dad's favorite bread, pizza and salads. As I looked at the small group of family and friends, I felt so very lucky to have had this year with my dad. We were very much a team till the end.

Thank you for all of your love, support and kindness during this last year. It has taken me all these four and a half months to write the last chapter because it still feels so raw—missing Dad and the last 5 days. With so much gratitude & love, Suzie

On Death - Gibran

You would know the secret of death. But how shall you find it unless you seek it in the heart of life? The owl whose night-bound eyes are blind unto the day cannot unveil the mystery of light. If you would indeed behold the spirit of death, open your heart wide unto the body of life. For life and death are one, even as the river and the sea are one.

In the depth of your hopes and desires lies your silent knowledge of the beyond; And like seeds dreaming beneath the snow your heart dreams of spring. Trust the dreams, for in them is hidden the gate to eternity. Your fear of death is but the trembling of the shepherd when he stands before the king whose hand is to be laid upon him in honour. Is the shepherd not joyful beneath his trembling, that he shall wear the mark of the king? Yet is he not more mindful of his trembling?

For what is it to die but to stand naked in the wind and to melt into the sun? And what is it to cease breathing, but to free the breath from its restless tides, that it may rise and expand and seek God unencumbered?

Only when you drink from the river of silence shall you indeed sing. And when you have reached the mountain top, then you shall begin to climb. And when the earth shall claim your limbs, then shall you truly dance.

-- Kahlil Gibran

About the Author

Suzie Abels is also the author of *Kindness on a Budget*, which illustrates the gifts of being kind daily, both for the giver and the receiver alike. She has discussed her book on numerous radio shows and has appeared as a featured guest speaker at Soul of Yoga, Seventh Chakra Yoga, Peace Prayer Day in Los Angeles, and has addressed The Guru Ram Das Ashram, sharing the value of kindness in one's path. A public speaker, she also offers private sessions on how to follow your heart in all of life's matters.

The mother of three, she resides with her husband of 30 years, Peter, in California where they enjoy hiking and gardening.

www.ingramcontent.com/pod-product-compliance
Lightning Source LLC
La Vergne TN
LVHW091218080426
835509LV00009B/1057